Black and Blue: The Color of Love

Based on a true story

Black and Blue: The Color of Love

Based on a true story

By

Autumn Toth

ISBN# 1-58500-841-9

ABOUT THE BOOK

"Black and Blue: The Color of Love?" you ask yourself. "How do these colors relate to love?" you ponder.

For many these are the only colors of love they know. These are the colors of the wounds left from a battle ground where the only expression of love is through a fist of abusive words. They are symbolic of a life of violence, darkening the soul and discoloring the flesh.

Louise, a college student at Cal. State San Bernadino, worked two jobs, but always found time to participate in a few extra curricular activities. Where men were concerned, she had a history of falling for the "underdog"-usually handsome men, but were coined "losers." But, she was always able to see the kindness in their hearts under the masks they wore, and "Save Me" signs on their foreheads. Underneath the tough exterior Louise presented to the world, all she longed for was to be loved, accepted and needed by someone special. She used whatever she could get her hands on as a means to fill her emptiness.

Larry was no exception, but in the end, it was Louise who needed to be saved. She encountered him in a bar late one evening in December 1990. He was a blast from her past; their paths had not crossed for years. His sign was displayed in neon which hooked her instantly. She sauntered over to where he was sitting and reacquainted herself with him. She then proceeded to get his phone number before they parted that evening. She telephoned him several weeks later, and from that day forward, her life took an unexpected turn.

Louise's world quickly dissolved and became his world. They laughed, cried, fought, made love and partied together. As her love intensified, the need to save him from himself became her primary purpose. Then the beatings began.

Louise moved in with Larry and the spiral into darkness and despair became the evident path. The abuse was frequent, usually every few days. He laced her food with PCP, and for days she teetered on the brink of sanity, sometimes stepping with both feet in the world of the insane. Love and hate melded together in a synnymous feeling, for her towards Larry.

She managed to find a glimmer of light and strength in a world she had come to believe impermeable to anything other than the microcosm that had been created with Larry. On November 15, 1991, she took a stand for the only person she could help, herself. A shattered shell of a women laid at her feet. From the debris and wreckage arose a child determined, angry and fighting to b free.

I write this book not only for myself, but for every person who may find themselves in volatile situations unable to see away to change there circumstances. There is a way to create a life filled with joy.

And just as the mighty Phoenix has risen from the ashes, symbolic of its past. In a powerful upward surge that signifies a freedom that can only be the result of deep and abiding internal transformation. So has Autumn Toth, been lifted from the horrid depths of her own tumultuous history only to begin ascending the rungs of the spiritual ladder that exist within us all.

A NOTE TO THE READERS

This novel is the depiction of one woman's experience strictly, through her eyes. The location could have been anywhere and the individuals could have been anyone. As the author I made a random decision to choose an area of familiarity to me. Any correlation to any place or experience you may recognize is purely coincidental.

This novel does not adhere to strict rules of non fiction therefore it is claimed to be a work of fiction.

ACKNOWLEDGMENTS

First and foremost I must say that without God in my life, who is a constant source of strength, courage and inspiration I would not be here to share this story.

I asked those of you who have chosen to read this book to please take a moment and read this section. The people I will mention in the following text have been instrumental in the fruition, some directly and others indirectly, of this book. They all hold a special place in my heart. They have brightened my life in otherwise shadowed and tragic periods. They have encouraged me in creating my own reality. They have constructively criticized me when I needed to hear that. But first and foremost they continue to love and care for me unconditionally with all my idiosyncrasies and unconventional ways.

I'd like to thank everyone at 1st books library for making this online publication possible, for their support and constant communication through this process.

My best friend for the last 18 years, my celestial sister, Becky McColley, who has walked a mile in my shoes with me when I needed her too. With whom I share a constant source of joy, laughter and tears. A woman with whom together we will never grow up, only a little wiser.

Ginny Schauburger, who generously supplied me with a computer printed the manuscript at various stages and who as read, read and read every piece of paper printed about this novel and continually encouraged me to follow my passion for writing and life. She continues and will always be one of the dearest friends I have the opportunity to share my life with.

Karen Winters, who has graciously opened her home to me and given me a safe place to write without interruption. Who has continually given of herself, her time, and her resources to her friends. I am so grateful to be one of those people.

G.W. Taylor for taking the time to write an outstanding and heartfelt bio for me. A man whose laughter and song always up lift everyone who hears them. His friendship has become a cherished gift in my life

John Bowen, whose friendship, kindness and generosity made this happen alot sooner than it may have.

My family, who has known me all my life and still love me. And I thank them for their continued support in my life.

My mom, who taught me to follow my heart, even when my choices seemed a bit unrealistic to everyone else. She is always there without fail in a world that can be stressful at times I can always count on her. She continues to teach me about staying connected and expanding my heart and mind to all the beautiful spectacular opportunities life has to offer .

My father who taught me how to make my dreams a reality and for being here for me.

My grandfather, who is no longer with us, but was and is always a constant source of love. An amazing storyteller and a caring, dedicated teacher. Through his actions he taught me how to live life and to love life and everything in it. He taught me to have faith and trust in my own knowing.

Dishwalla and Todd Snider & the Nervous Wrecks, whose music inspired and propelled me forward to complete the manuscript. I'd slip their CD's in when it became a difficult task to write this story and keep on writing. With great admiration and respect for their talent and the people in and behind the bands, I thank them.

I would also like to thank the people who are an active and important part of my life today. For their friendship, caring and time.

I thank each and every one of you for taking the time to read this book. Enjoy.

In The End

The sky was gray and ominous on this November morning, revealing neither sun nor rain. The early morning fog had begun to lift from the valley floor of Diamond Bar, California, but the bleakness of the day remained.

Diamond Bar was located fifty miles south from the base of the San Bernardino Mountains and forty miles north of Huntington Beach; an ideal location for some, a prison for others. The town was situated between the hills, creating a basin encumbered with a dense haze in the winter and smog in the summer. A dark cloud seemed to hover over Diamond Bar year around. The forces that lurked within its boundaries fed on the vulnerability of those who chose to live within its reach, slowly draining the life out of its victims. People flocked there to partake of the beautiful rolling hills, the vast undeveloped countryside and the many business opportunities. For me, the town and the people carried with it memories of a nightmare I never want to relive.

I drove south on Diamond Bar Blvd, in a small blue Ford pick up. My destination: freedom. Turning left on Castle Rock, I could see the two-story white colonial home at the end of the cul-de-sac. Weather beaten and worn the shutters hung loosely on their hinges, clashing against the window from the force of the wind. The windows facing the street had been vandalized; where glass used to reside, foil now lived. The exterior paint was chipping and peeling, leaving areas of bare wood exposed. Many of the shingles on the roof had deteriorated causing leaks in the interior during heavy rains.

A foreboding feeling arose in my gut, like a Mt. St. Helen on the verge of eruption. I parallel parked the truck along the curb in front of the house. I hesitated in the cab. Looking through the windshield, I scanned the intersection. From my parking place at the end of the cul-de-sac I could see the ARCO station to my left. Directly in front of my view was an undeveloped field consisting of dirt and weeds. The city had proposed to turn the vacant lot into small park sometime in the future. If I looked past the field on the other side of Diamond Bar Blvd. a small liquor store was set on the northeast corner amongst a few vacant shops and a pay phone in the parking lot. Directly across from the store was a Shell gas station. The streets seemed unnaturally desolate. I inhaled deeply and reached inside myself to gather every ounce of courage to face the task at hand.

As I stepped out of the truck, the cold breeze hit my face. The wind pushed at my back as I headed for the front door. The foundation felt like it was crumbling beneath my feet. The lawn, no longer lush and green, was overrun by devil's grass. A brick wall encased the planter, the mortar that held the wall in place was disintegrating. The rose bushes that once flourished there, their scent oh, so sweet, were now dead. No chirping of birds, no roar of engines could be heard in my ears. I lingered on the porch for what seemed like an eternity, dressed in a size three pair of Paris Blues straight legged jeans that were held up only by my protruding hip bones. I had lost close to ten pounds over the last few months which was not quite a tenth of my entire body weight. I remembered the last time I looked in the mirror while I was living in this house. As I looked through my vacant eyes, the only vision that stared back at me was one of self-deprecation. "What was happening to me?" I thought to myself, "My physical appearance only denotes to the world the emotional bankruptcy that has taken place inside of me." A black mid riff sleeveless T-shirt covered my chest along with a large blue and black man's flannel that hung past my ass.

I searched the recesses of my mind back to a time when I thought I was in control of my life. How had my life ever become so unmanageable? Lost. Spending most of my youth buried in books, writing in my diary, listening and dancing to my mother's eight tracks, I spent little time cultivating my common sense. Raped at the age of thirteen, I turned to anything that would take away the pain and shame. I replayed the events of the last year over in my mind as I stood on the doorstep, prolonging the inevitable.

It was shortly after 1:00 a.m., I was intoxicated and at the peak of my high. The night was just beginning, according to my internal clock, but the Tree House Nightclub would be closing soon. I had spent a good portion of the evening downstairs socializing with two tall, dark haired attractive men. We drank and danced, laughed and drank, and drank some more. I made it a policy never to remember the strangers' names that I met in bars. Generic names such as "Babe" and "Hon" were sufficient, and this nonchalant, detached attitude kept me impermeable to feeling.

The Tree House Nightclub was located on North Diamond Bar Blvd. next door to the only bowling alley in town. The bar was two stories. The first floor was littered with black lights that hid the extensive amount of dirt ground into the burnt orange carpet. Once inside, there were many options to choose from. At the south end of the first floor was a raised stage live music was performed there five nights a week. A dance floor sat beneath the stage. To the right of the entryway were two electronic dartboards, which ninety percent of the night were in use. There were an abundance of tables located on the bottom level. A bar that stretched fifteen feet across the west wall was brightly lit by neon beer and spirit signs. To the left of the entrance was a staircase leading to the second floor. At the top of the stairs, a small service bar, with five stools in front of it, lay to the left along with the rest rooms past the bar. To the right, three pool tables were horizontally aligned, and the felt that covered the tabletops was stained with alcohol. Bright fluorescent lights hung above each table so the players could clearly see their shots. The design was such that from the seats, one could look over the railing to observe what was happening below.

I tilted my head toward the upstairs and caught a glimpse of some familiar faces, Darin, Danny and Larry, seated along the railing. Danny had been a constant friend and ex-lover. He stood 5' 10" with short brown hair and small, round brown eyes with gold flecks throughout the iris. He had a medium build, but when he drank continuously for days his abdomen expanded. If he'd been a woman, an onlooker would have considered him pregnant. That was the only part of his body that outwardly showed the effects of his drinking. I had only met Darin briefly through mutual friends. He was a handsome Hispanic man with wavy dark hair and green eyes. The man that caught my eye was Larry Jennings.

I met Larry eight years ago. My family and I had moved from Glendora to Diamond Bar the summer between my sophomore and junior year. It was the first day of my junior year at Diamond Bar High School when we met. We hung out, drank and snorted lines together until he was expelled from school shortly into the academic year. Our brief friendship disappeared with his expulsion. Our paths crossed periodically without acknowledgment, by either of us, that at one time we had been friends. I was preparing for marriage and college while he was still the same guy I had met in high school. It had been three years since the last time we encountered one another.

Tonight there was something different about him. Maybe it was the mischievous glimmer in his beautiful blue eyes that sparked an interest in me. I decided to simply reacquaint myself with Larry. I excused myself from my present company and sauntered across the room and up the stairs, attracting wanton stares. I was clad in my three-inch high black pumps, a tight black mini skirt that hung just below my bottom, a sheer white blouse and a small black hand bag draped over my shoulder.

Arriving at their table, I stood between Darin and Danny. I wrapped my arms around each of their shoulders and gave them both a peck on the cheek.

" How are you ,boys?"

Not giving either of them a chance to reply, I looked at Larry, who was sitting directly across from his friends. I flashed a warm, seductive smile his direction. His fine blonde hair cascaded down his shoulders and his boyish features gave him the appearance of innocence. He stood about 5'11" with a slender lean build. I was completely captivated by his charming good looks.

" How are you ,Larry? It's been a long time."

" Too long, Louise," he replied.

" What is happening after the club closes tonight?" I inquired.

" Stop by my house if you like, I'm having a little after hours party. Do you remember where I live?"

" I think so."

" Let me give you my phone number just in case."

He then proceeded to write his number on a cocktail napkin and handed it to me. Slipping the number in my purse, I said " I'll see you guys later." I returned to my evenings companions.

I explained to my new found friends of the evening that I did not drive to the bar. I convinced them to drive me to the south end of town, to Larry's house. Last call was being made, and while most of the patrons were scampering to the bar to purchase their last cocktail of the evening, the two men and I vacated the premises to the parking lot. We hopped into a silver Acura, drove to the south end in search of Larry's pad, but to no avail. We decided to go back to the driver's house and continue the merriment.

-2-

The bedroom window faced to the west. The rising sun pierced through the windowpane, awakening me from sleep. I cupped my temples in the palm of my hands, hoping the pressure would be relieved, and I squeezed my eyes shut to block out the morning light. A hazy vision of the night before swirled in my mind. I opened my eyes and surveyed the room. The bedroom was decorated in deep, rich maple wood, and forest green was the color dominating the room. The room had a definite masculine affectation. Who was this naked man lying naked next to me? It was a question that did not concern me for more than a moment. I had long since stopped being shocked by my actions.

Careful not to make a sound, I slipped out of bed, gathered my clothes and slipped them on, carrying my high heels in my hand. I tiptoed over to the chair where his pants hung and searched his pockets for his wallet. Finding the wallet, I took just enough money for a cab ride home and checked his driver's license in order to get the address for the cab company. Placing the wallet back in his pants pocket, I managed to leave the bedroom without disturbing him. I called the local cab company to drive me home.

"To the Galleria apartments on North Street in Anaheim, please," I told the cab driver.

Arriving at my apartment complex, which I shared with two other girls, Janis and Carol, who were out of town for the weekend, I headed straight for the elevator. The complex was three stories, four buildings. They were arranged in a manner that created a large rectangular courtyard in the middle with all the amenities one could ask for. A gym, jacuzzi, pool and gas grills. We lived on the second floor, in the building furthest from the office, building four. The laundry room was directly across the hall from our front door. All the apartments were reached by walking down brightly lit corridors. It was designed much like a hotel. The carpet that was throughout the building was a dingy brown seventies style covering.

I entered the apartment which was a three bedroom, two bath floor plan. I went directly to my room, which was the master. The room was the shape of a block letter "J," with the long end being unproportionately wide. On the north wall, the top of the "J," an oversized window stretched from floor to ceiling to allow sunlight in. On the south wall, the base of the "J," parallel with the door was a computer desk and computer. The shelves were filled with college textbooks. Past the desk, in the upswing portion of the "J," was a small dressing area with a sink, closets and a full bath. On the east wall was a synthetic, dark wood wall unit that housed the TV and fiction novels. A day bed was positioned directly across from the TV which was covered in soft yellow floral print comforter and dust ruffle. Four pillows, all covered with matching yellow shams, were placed erect along the back of the bed. The frame was painted white and had a high back and gold balls on the top of each post. An old brown vinyl beanbag rested near the window.

I dropped my shoes and purse on the floor and turned on the TV. I had no desire to watch it, I only wanted the background noise. Silence was deafening to my senses. Without the distraction, my thoughts would begin to scream out to me, trying to purge my soul of the garbage I had taken such care to bury deep inside me. The pains of the past. The sound of my parents arguing through closed doors about my father's mistress. I did not understand my father's blatant adultery. At an early age I translated it into reasons I could understand. "I was a bad girl, and that is why Daddy behaves the way he does." I convinced myself. Then, I was raped by two boys I thought were my friends. Denials, shame and hurt were all subdued by anything that quieted the voices. It was easier to run than to face the events and emotions of the past.

I moved towards the mirror. My hair was disheveled and my clothes wrinkled with stains from last night's cocktails. I let the clothes fall from my body to the floor. I went to the bathroom and began running hot water for a bath. Standing before the mirror, eyeing my slender nude figure, I caressed my supple breast then ran my hands down my sternum across my rib cage to my stomach, along the thin trail of hair that extended from my chest to my pubic hair. The skin against my fingertips was soft to the touch. My body was slender and curvy, but with no real muscle definition. This physical exploration had become a ritual. I caught the reflection of my face, worn and tired for a woman of twenty-three. My large brown eyes stared vacantly back at me. Residue of last night's make up was smeared across my face, and I had dark circles beneath my eyes from the smudged mascara. The sound of the water beginning to flow onto the bathroom floor jolted me from my self-observation. Turning the bath water off and mopping the over flow up with a towel, I cautiously dipped my toes into the almost scalding water, then eased my entire body into the tub. Steam rose above my head and luxuriously soothed my aching body. I sunk completely under the water in order to moisten myself from head to toe. The bath was purifying and removed all traces of the night's excursion off my skin. Bringing myself to the surface, I leaned back against the end of the tub, closed my eyes, and drifted off into another world.

Everything was black. There was blood splashed against the backdrop. A woman was screaming in the distance. A hand large enough to hold a human in its palm. Sharp pointed nails protruded from the fingertips. Thick, coarse dark hair covered the back of the hand, the skin beneath was aged and rough. The screams came from inside the clenched fist. Slowly the hand opened. I stared at myself lying motionless clothed in blood, in the palm of the demon hand.

Paralyzed in the nightmare, I struggled to wake up. Coming out of my dream state, eyelids opening, I realized I had become chilled. The bath water felt like ice against my prune like skin. Shreds of the nightmare still lingered in my mind as I stepped out of the bath. I reached for the towel that hung, as I tried to forget the nightmare.

-3-

The nap I took was sufficient to clear the cob webs from my brain. Peering out my window, I noticed night had fallen over the city. Time to study. I gathered my textbooks and lecture notes and began the first day of what would be a week long cram session, in order to prepare for finals. This final's week was like any other in my college career. Previewing and reviewing lecture notes, reading and rereading text books, and attending group study sessions that would last into the early morning hours. After a week of intense studying I felt confident I would ace my exams. A bright, intelligent woman with an above average I. Q., I had always done well in academics, but the same could not be said of my knowledge of life. My lack of experience and know-it-all attitude would someday cost me.

I attended Cal State San Bernardino. I was about to complete the fall quarter of my junior year. I was studying accounting, working towards a BS in that field. My goal was to become a CPA.. The campus was nestled at the base of the San Bernardino Mountains. The grounds were sprawling. The lawns always green and well manicured. If the sun was radiant and hot, the students could find relief under one of the many and various trees on the school grounds. I found it more enjoyable to hang out in the campus pub and pool hall, which was really just a cafeteria that served draft beer and had two pool tables.

I completed my finals with flying colors. The quarter was over and it was Christmas break. I bid my fellow classmates farewell until next semester. Shouting, " May Santa be good to you," I skipped gleefully off campus as finishing finals was cause for celebration.

4

I captured the holiday spirit with full force. I spent the holiday break working, shopping, visiting family and attending festive parties.

I was employed in the service industry. I waited tables and cocktailed at El Gato Gordo in Riverside. The restaurant was located a couple miles south of the University of Riverside in the "red light district", as my co-workers and I affectionately called it. At night from the bar patio we would watch the hookers strolling up and down waiting for their next "John". After a day at school I would come to work in the evenings. I worked at El Gato Gordo three days a week.

I also worked part time managing and waiting tables, usually on the weekends, at the Whole Enchilada in Diamond Bar. R&M Food Services had employed me, which is the corporation the restaurant is owned by, since 1986. Although I had long periods of absence because I moved out of the area, I always came back. The restaurant was like my second home. The Whole Enchilada had been open only a short time when I first was hired. I had the opportunity to watch and be part of the growth and success of the business.

Both restaurants specialized in Mexican food. The morale and camaraderie between the employees and management was excellent. That created a fun and enjoyable working atmosphere, one that made me enjoy going to work. During the holidays, the customers were always a little more generous with gratuities than at any other time of the year. If available, I would pick up a few extra shifts during Christmas break. A little extra cash never hurt for those shopping expeditions.

I partook in both company Christmas parties and any others I was invited to. My roommates and I had a small, intimate tree trimming party.

Janis, Carol, and I purchased a Douglas fir Christmas tree to place in our unfurnished living room. We had very few store bought ornaments and even less disposable cash to decorate the tree. In order to properly decorate it in the spirit of the season, we popped popcorn, strung it on a fishing line, and then wrapped it around the tree in place of traditional garland. Previously, I had gathered pinecones from one of the mountain hikes I went on. I placed makeshift bows, made from red cloth ribbon, on each cone, and hung them sporadically on the branches. We did make a group decision to all pitch in on some twinkle lights, because Christmas without a brightly-lit tree standing in the middle of a barren living room just wasn't Christmas. Placing the last strand of lights on the tree Janis, plugged them in. We all stood back to take in the full view of our artistic creation. Glancing at each other we suddenly burst into laughter. Laughing hysterically we fell to the floor clutching our stomachs. The tree looked ridiculous. A pine cone here and there, popcorn strands drooping on the outer edge of the branches, various types of store bought ornaments hanging with no particular order. The lights were so bright and so numerous that they dwarfed the five-foot tree, but it was ours, and we loved every last pine needle.

We decided to exchange gifts, since it was Christmas Eve. First, we all settled in to smoke a joint and partake in a glass of holiday nog. The agreement was to spend a maximum of five dollars per person. We each gave our gifts to the others. Giggling and ripping wrapping paper, we opened our presents.

Janis received a white T-shirt with small pink pigs drawn on the front from Carol. I gave her a comical ceramic cowpig piggy bank dressed in a dark blue cowboy hat, eyes that were far too large for its head. Carol received a pair of crystal champagne glasses from me, a purchase that exceeded our agreement, but on a prior date I had carelessly broken one of her glasses. Also, a pair of thong back panties from Janis, because she was always bragging she had the most experience of the three of us between the sheets. I received a winter hat from Carol that she had made out of a pair of old black sweats, and a simple black fitted T-shirt from Janis.

Raising our glasses to toast, Carol said, " May we all use our gifts in good health and in naughty deeds."

We wrapped up the evening passing around a doobie and sharing stories of lurid sexual fantasies. Janis and Carol both shared stories that included unattainable men, while I on the other hand shared a story of a more realistic nature. I shared with my friends the brief encounter with Larry in the bar and what I desired to do with him. High and ready for sleep, we hugged one another and thanked each for the gifts we had received. We headed for bed, where we all slept undisturbed until Christmas morning.

Each of us awoke ready for the day's events with family and friends. I borrowed a floral pants suit to wear, which was rich in deep purple and green flowers against a black background. Underneath the jacket, I wore a black sleeveless camisole. I admired my choice of attire in the mirror. I looked radiant today. Large brown eyes with hint of pale pink shadow, thick long eye lashes once the mascara was applied, small shapely red lips, and high cheek bones, my features all characteristic of my Hungarian heritage. My hair was thick, long and sandy blonde. It fell to the middle of my back. I exited my bedroom to find Janis. Janis was in her bathroom putting on her final touches for the day. Not only was she one of my best friends, she was also my hairdresser.

"Janis, do you have time to French braid my hair?"

" Sure, let's do it right now. Come sit down," she said, motioning to the toilet lid.

Janis was very skilled at her craft and completed my hair in a matter of five minutes.

" Where's Carol?"

"She already left for her mom's," Janis replied.

I stood, kissed Janis on the cheek, wished her a merry Christmas and left the apartment.

It was a cool sunny winter day. There was not a cloud to be seen in the blue sky above. I drove to Azusa to spend the day with my father and stepfamily. I was greeted warmly when I arrived. We spent the day feasting, drinking and catching up on each other's lives. It was a wonderful day.

5

The week passed into next year. I attended one party after another. A couple of days into the new year I decided to call Larry Jennings. Sunrays entered through my window, warming my flesh as I lay on my day bed turning his number over in my palm. I rehearsed in my mind the direction I wished to carry the conversation before picking up the receiver and dialing. It was ringing.

" Hello?," someone answered.

" Is Larry home?" I asked.

" This is he."

"Hi, it's Louise. How are you?"

We talked idly for a few moments before I asked Larry what his plans for the day were.

" I have some errands to run, would like to join me?" he asked.

" Sounds like a plan. I'll meet you at your house in an hour. What is your address?"

After receiving his address I hung up the receiver and I contemplated what to wear. I decided on a pair of loose 501's and a midriff, button front, pastel pink sweater. Before leaving the apartment, I added a bit of color to my lips and mascara to my lashes. My hair flowed freely down my back moving with the wind as I walked to my Camaro RS. I inhaled the fresh afternoon air. There wasn't a trace of smog in the sky. I arrived at Larry's within the hour. I parked my car and proceeded up the walk to the front door.

The house was painted white with a midnight blue trim. The front consisted of well manicured hedges and a mossy ground cover everywhere the concrete was not. Six Large pillars supported the awning and carport that shaded the front of the house. To the right of the walk way stood a ceramic bird bath and fountain. A Greek statue pouring water from a pitcher into the pond was perched at the edge of the bath.

Before I could reach the front door, Larry stepped onto the porch and greeted me with a warm, friendly hug. He wore a pair of

Levi's, T-shirt with the Nike emblem on the chest and pair of Nike running shoes. Ironically, years before I had written Larry off as a loser. Sure, he was attractive enough, but he seemed to be headed on a path of self destruction. My, how views can change when you look from a different angle. Now I would enter his lair.

" Come in," he said

I followed him through the foyer to a staircase on my left. I noticed the entrance was decorated with gold leaf mirrored tiles which covered the wall and a Greek statue sat on the entry table to my right. A gaudy Mediterranean motif was displayed in the decor throughout the house, with the exception of Larry's bedroom. My feet sank in the red carpet as I walked up the stair case. He led me to his bedroom, which was on the second floor facing the street. It was an average size room with modest decor. A desk and a double bed on the east wall, an array of different car models on the bookshelves near the window on the west wall, and a small round night table dressed in a blue cloth and a glass top was positioned near the head of the bed filled the room.

Telling me to make myself at home, he sat at the head of the bed and pulled a small ziplock bag from his pocket. It contained a pinkish powdery substance. My eyes widened. He sensed my anticipation. A smile formed on his lips. He dumped a teaspoon full of the contents on to the glass top night stand. Tap, tap, tap, the sound of the razor blade meeting the glass rung in my ears.

He turned to me and asked, "Would you like one?" while with a couple of flicks of the wrist he expertly drew two lines.

I nodded my head in affirmation. He held out a small straw and motioned for me to go ahead. I walked over to the table, I took the straw from his hand, bent down and inhaled. I could taste the bitterness in my mouth as the chemicals coursed through my body. I felt exhilarated. Larry then followed my lead.

We decided to go to the Brea Mall so Larry could exchange a Christmas gift. We exited his house, jumped in his truck and left Diamond Bar. We spent a good portion of the afternoon shopping and talking. Our appetites having returned, we stopped at the Taco Bell near the mall. We went inside to order. I ordered a red burrito and a taco. Larry had a much larger appetite, and ordered a six pack of tacos and a burrito supreme. We took our food and sat outside on the patio to enjoy the winter sun. Returning to the truck after lunch, he handed me his stash.

" Go for it," he said, giving me a cassette case, " use this."

Placing a small amount on the hard plastic cover, I drew up a couple lines using a credit card. I rolled up a bill, and placing it in my right nostril, inhaled deeply rewarded with an immediate rush. I gagged when the drug hit the back of my throat, the drip. A small price to pay to feel whole. I passed the case over to Larry and held onto to the steering wheel so he could do his.

"Ahhhh, what do you say we get some beer and go over to my cousin's house."

" Sounds great," I replied

After stopping at the liquor store we drove to La Mirada, where we spent the rest of the day drinking and shooting the shit with his cousin, Johnny and his friends. Johnny was a short, red headed man with freckles and light colored skin. His eyes were green. He was obviously Irish. As an objective observer it was difficult for me to discern whether or not Johnny liked his cousin. Most comments from Johnny towards or to Larry were back handed compliments or insults camouflaged in a joke. As the day turned into night we made our way back to Larry's house.

-6-

When we arrived back at Larry's, his sister Jan was waiting for him, as were a dozen phone messages. Jan was a hefty woman in her mid thirties with mousy brown hair without style or shape. Her eyes were almond shaped and brown in color. The blue jeans she wore looked painted on with an oversized T-shirt hanging over her belly. She looked nothing like her brother. Larry's sister took on the responsibility of keeping an eye on him since his mother's death a year prior. Greeting his sister, he then introduced her to me.

While Larry returned phone calls, Jan and I chatted. Jan expressed a grave concern about Larry's activities. I listened intently in hopes of understanding this man. Different friends soon began arriving. Some only stayed a moment, while others stayed long enough to drink a beer.

Craving a cigarette and feeling a bit suffocated, I excused myself and stepped outside into the night air. I sat on the front step, lit a smoke and inhaled deeply. Looking out towards the street I relished the opportunity to be outside. Two familiar vehicles pulled up to the house. Inside them were Mitch, the husband from whom I had recently separated, in a raised silver Nissan 4x4, and Danny, in a raised red Toyota 4x4 with a shell. Danny was the man fore whom I had left Mitch for. He was also Mitch's best friend. Sitting in the shadows, I thought sarcastically to myself, "what a cozy scene", and pondered for a moment why neither of these men were a romantic part of my life, now. Mitch was my high school sweetheart, in a pubescent state of confusion at the age of fifteen, through a teenagers eyes, he was my prince. As the years accumulated in our relationship, the struggle inside me grew increasingly more turbulent, I needed to break the mold that was not me. I tried for seven years to become what I thought others expected, marriage, college degree, house, dogs and working to have kids. I only knew one way at that time to break free, which was to involve myself with another man. Danny was merely a catalyst in that transitory period of my life. A residual of love resided inside my heart for both these men. The man that took me to heaven, the man that brought me back to earth and the man that would take me to ?.... all together under one roof. One big happy family. When the two men reached the porch where I was sitting, we all greeted each other. Neither seemed surprised that I was there.

I saw sadness in Mitch's gentle blue eyes, maybe for a marriage that would never be, with a woman he would always love. Mitch was an inch shorter than I was with a stocky build and broad shoulders tapering down to his waist line. His chest was covered in blonde hair and strong athletic legs. His tight curly blonde hair, cut over his ears and came just above his shirt collar. Mitch's choice of dress was always consistent: blue jeans and a T-shirt in the cooler months, and shorts and T-shirt in the warmer periods.

We all walked into the house together to find Larry. We headed up the stairs. Larry was sitting busily in front of his night stand. We all sat on the bed and talked as if nothing had ever been shared between us, other than a deep affection of friendship. Mitch and Danny departed after they got what they came for.

While this was taking place, Jan remained in the kitchen and attempted to remain oblivious to Larry's business.

After the business was taken care of and the crowd dispersed, we returned downstairs. Jan acted very agitated. With concern and anger in her voice, she spoke to Larry about his so-called business.

" Don't you understand if you continue to do this and the police catch you we could lose everything Mom left us?"

Larry became very distraught over the mention of his mother. Tears filled his eyes. He tried to explain to Jan that he had been looking for a regular job and what he was doing was just temporary. This was the only way he could pay the bills.

" You never complain when you come to me for cash, so please don't start now," he retorted

This display of vulnerability and emotion by Larry screamed to my caretaker instincts. I felt the need to wrap my arms around him and comfort him. Instead, I just listened.

Larry turned to me. He pleaded for me to take him away from his house, to a place we wouldn't be disturbed. No reminders of his Mom. No phone calls. No other people.

" O.K., we'll go back to my apartment," I said.

Larry and I stood to leave. First, I assured Jan everything would be all right and not to worry about Larry tonight.

On the drive to Anaheim, Larry regained his composure. Since the night I encountered Larry in the bar I had fantasized about doing wild wonderful things with him and to him. This was a golden opportunity for me to fulfill my lustful desires. My body yearned to feel his manhood deep inside of me. I wanted to love him. To save him.

-7-

When we reached my apartment my roommates were home. I introduced Larry to Janis and Carol then quickly whisked him away to my bedroom and closed the bedroom door. I stood in front of Larry and placed my arms around his neck. He lifted my face to his and kissed my lips. He aroused a passion deep inside my soul.

Withdrawing from our kiss I said, " What do you say we get comfortable?"

Without waiting for an answer, I removed myself from his embrace, lit three candles and turned off the light. Seductively, I slipped off my jeans and sweater, leaving only my bra and panties on. I gave him a moment to take in the view before lying down on the carpet. Playfully, I patted the empty space beside me.

" What do you say, sexy, care to join me?"

I could see the outline of his hard cock pressed against the inner seam of his blue jeans. I could feel the wetness between my thighs. I watched silently as he removed his clothing with an air of confidence. He knelt down next to me and slipped the lace cup of the bra below my nipple while lowering his mouth to my breast. I felt shivers run along my entire body. My hand ran down his smooth muscular chest to his groin. I wrapped my hand around the shaft of his cock and began slowly moving it up and down. I pressed my body against his, slipping my hand away and around his neck. I could feel his hardness against my pelvis. His hands felt every inch of my flesh.

" Fuck me." I whispered in his ear " I want to feel you inside me."

Nudging him to lay on his back, I stood on my knees and straddled his body. I lowered myself on top of him. He glided inside me and I moved my body up and down. Unexpectedly, he went limp. Breaking the connection between us, I eased off and moved down his body. I reached the lower part of his body and drew him into my mouth. I swirled my tongue around the head then took him deep into the back of my throat. The attempt to arouse him proved in vain. I did not understand this turn of events as I had always had the power to arouse men. My ego was crushed. This ordeal made me more determined than ever to pursue Larry.

Apologizing profusely, Larry wrapped his arms around me.

" It is not you, I have a lot on my mind and sometimes 'the pink' makes it impossible for me to stay hard."

That did little to console my bruised ego. He lay quietly on his back. I rested my head on his chest and draped my leg over his body. With his arms wrapped around my torso, we drifted off to sleep. I tossed and turned by his side.

I felt his finger tips moving slowly and methodically along my inner thigh as I began to wake from the netherworld. His lips kissed the nape of my neck. I began to respond to his touch. I glanced toward the window and saw that darkness still cloaked the city. Turning my face towards his, we kissed. He slipped inside of me. We made love until the early morning hours. Sweaty and satisfied, we drifted back to sleep.

-8-

I awoke shortly before noon to find the sun beating through my bedroom window. He lay peacefully beside me, his appearance angelic and his skin soft and creamy white. A thin, short scar was the only evidence on his face of reconstructive surgery, the consequence of an adolescent game of chicken when he was seventeen. I kissed him tenderly on the forehead. Slowly he began to wake up and opened his translucent blue eyes. A sheepish smile flashed across his face, revealing white, perfectly straight teeth. He looked into my dark smoldering eyes. Our eyes lingered upon one another for a brief moment as tenderness passed between us.

Kissing me, he asked, " Are you hungry?"

"Yes," I replied.

"How about I go and get something for us to eat?"

"O.K." I said, as I pointed to my keys.

He slipped out from beneath my arm that was draped over his bare chest. My gaze followed his lean, muscular naked body as he put on his clothes. Dressed in last night's faded blue jeans and T-shirt, he headed for the door.

"I'll be right back."

The door closed behind him.

I lingered on my bed, recapturing the rhapsody that had taken me into dimensions not of this world. My mind filled with thoughts of what the future might bring for Larry and me. I had a tendency to plummet into a world of romance, which rendered me incapable of common sense. I wanted this man in my life. Visions of making love, sharing a walk on the beach and holding hands connected as one played on my mental screen. I ran my hands over my bare breast. My nipples hardened. I moved my finger tips down my abdomen to the thick coarse dark pubic hair where only hours before Larry had traced my body with his gentle touch.

Hearing him return, I jumped off the bed and slipped a light wrap that hung mid thigh around my body. I walked from my room into the dining room, an empty space with no table or chairs, only a 1970's light fixture hung from the ceiling. Making use of what I had available, I grabbed a large beach towel from the counter that was there for just such an occasion. I unfolded it and placed on the floor under the chandelier. I went to the kitchen and removed two forks from the drawer and grabbed two root beers from the refrigerator. Returning to the dining area, I placed them on opposite sides of the towel.

Larry called Darin to pick him up from the apartment and take him to his truck, while I set up the eating area. When I was finished, I waved Larry over to bring the food and have a seat.

I was unaware that I was so ravished until I began to devour my El Pollo chicken burrito. We ate without conversation as a silent calm that filled the room. After completing our meal, we looked up at each other at the exact same moment and burst into laughter. Realizing for those minutes in which we ate, we had become completely oblivious to the other ones presence.

Once the laughter subsided, Larry bent toward me. I could feel his breath on my face. The smell of cilantro and onion permeated my senses as he kissed me.

"I'll call you later," he said, as he stood up and headed for the front door.

I began straightening up the apartment. My body moved through the motions as I picked up the dirty clothes, threw them in the hamper, made my daybed, washed the dirty dishes, and vacuumed the carpet. All the while, I seemed to be on the outside looking in.

My mind still seemed a bit foggy, as if in a trance. My heartbeat became erratic as visions of Larry danced in my thoughts. A burning desire to feel Larry inside me occupied my mind. My desire for Larry was so intense , so passionate and so needy which was so out of character for me. "What is happening?" I asked myself.

College would be starting next week. I brought my mind back to the present. I needed to purchase supplies and books before the quarter began. I jotted a list on paper and formulated in my mind the route I would take to complete my errands as I dressed. Grabbing my purse off the dresser, I left the apartment, leaving behind the memories of last night.

I left for school early Tuesday morning. My first class, music appreciation, was at 8:00 a.m. I had scheduled my classes in such a manner that I would only have to be on campus two days a week from 8:00 a.m. to 4:00 p.m., Tuesdays and Thursdays. In the evenings after classes I went to work at El Gato Gordo. My shift started at 5:00 p.m. and lasted until approximately 10:00 p.m. My week was fairly routine.

My core classes for my major, accounting, were always the most difficult for me. Fortunately, I had the same professors this quarter as I'd, had last. I was familiar with their teaching and testing styles. Throughout my school career, I was always able to build a good rapport with my professors, getting to know them on a first name basis. I found sitting in the front row somehow gained respect, but more importantly kept me focused on the lecture. Taxing my mind was something I thirsted for. Attempting to earn a BS in accounting seemed to earn my father's respect and admiration, which I had been trying to do since my youth. Learning would hopefully keep my mind occupied with little time for thoughts of Larry, although periodically an image of him fluttered in mind.

The first week of classes introduced me to what I believed would be a challenging quarter. I was, without exception enthused about my classes and the thought of coming that much closer to a degree.

-12-

The week passed without incident or communication from Larry, until Friday. I returned home from work late Friday night to find a message from Larry on my answering machine. My heart skipped a beat as I listened to the message.

"Hi, Louise this is Larry. I was thinking about you so I thought I'd call and see if you wanted to spend some time together this weekend. Give me a call when you have chance. Any hour, day or night. I'll talk to you later." Without delay I returned his call.

"Hello."

"Hello, Larry?" I said questioningly

"No, this is Darin. Who is this?"

"Louise. Is Larry around?"

"Yeah, hang on I'll get him."

I waited patiently while Darin yelled for Larry. The butterflies were dancing in my stomach. Why was I so nervous? Jeez, I already passed the awkward stage of sex. Maybe it is because I care about this guy and I was afraid of being rejected. Before I had a chance to answer my own questions Larry's voice came booming through the receiver.

"Hey, how are you?"

"I'm fine. And you?"

"Great, thanks. So what are you doing this weekend?"

"Saturday I have to work until about 9:00 p.m. After that I don't have any plans."

"Well, what do you say after you finish your shift you come over to my house and from there we will figure out something to do?"

"Sounds great. I'll see you tomorrow night. Bye."

"Bye."

I held the receiver until I heard the dial tone singing in my ear.

I slipped out of my work uniform and prepared for bed. I was exhausted from the first week back in school, but at the same time anxious about tomorrow's date. I brushed my teeth, washed my face and put my hair in a pony tail. I was ready to slip into bed. My head lay on the pillow for what seemed like an eternity with a multitude of prospects and fantasies whirling around. The silence finally came with sleep close at its heels.

-13-

Fragments of a terrifying dream remained in my consciousness while I prepared myself for work. This nightmare left a haunting feeling inside me. "Why am I having nightmares?" I questioned silently to myself. "What was my subconscious trying to reveal to me, that I was blinded to in my waking hours?"

I outfitted myself in sexy, yet professional business attire, carefully applied my makeup, dried my hair and I was ready for work. Before leaving, I gathered a change of clothes for my evening with Larry then headed out the door.

The gray clouds were beginning to release the moisture that was stored within their confines. The roads were becoming slick from the first rain of the season. I drove cautiously north on the 57 freeway to Diamond Bar. I exited Grand. In matter of five minutes I was pulling into the back lot of The Whole Enchilada. By the time I arrived at work, all memories of the dream had been washed away.

I entered through the back door, went directly to the kitchen and poured myself a cup of coffee. I greeted the cooks on the line who were occupied doing the morning prep work, but each cheerfully acknowledged my greeting. The kitchen was divided from the service and dining area by a swinging door. I stepped through, coffee in hand, sipping cautiously to keep from burning my mouth. Instantly the caffeine alerted my brain cells to wake up. I walked to the cashier area and turned the register key to "Z". The machine began to spit out an itemized tape of last night's sales. While the register tape was printing, I opened the lock box, pulled out last night's drawer and the till for lunch. The registered beeped twice to signal it had completed the task. I placed the lunch till in the register, removed last nights tape and punched the day's date in its memory. Taking last night's till and the receipts, I headed back to the office to balance the books.

I found a certain amount of solace in counting the money and doing the books in the refuge of the office before we opened the doors for business. The paperwork typically took me about an hour and a half if there were no discrepancies. Today, there were no overages or shortages on the books. This part of the job was mechanical in nature, but I enjoyed calculating and balancing. It would be time to unlock the doors in about fifteen minutes. I locked the safe and slipped the paperwork in the desk. Leaning back in my chair, I pulled a cigarette from my pack and lit it. I could feel the tar enter into my lungs and the nicotine rush to my head. I enjoyed a smoke with a good cup of coffee.

The clock in the office struck 11:00 a.m.-- time to open. I would act as host and cashier until noon when Annette arrived to relieve me so I could carry out my management responsibilities. The duties were all encompassing, basically whatever needed to be done. Whether it was seating a guest, taking an order, making a margarita, dropping the overflow of cash from the register into the safe or making sure each customer was completely satisfied, I would do this until at least 9:00 in the evening.

The rain came down a good portion of the day, which always seemed to make for an excessively busy day. Today was no exception. The day passed quickly into evening. Finally the dinner crowd began to thin shortly after nine. I allowed the first two waitresses to begin their side work and stop taking tables. I made one last drop for the evening and turned the floor over to Suzy, the closing waitress and a very good friend.

I grabbed my change of clothes, a beer and headed for the ladies room to change. The excitement and anticipation of seeing Larry was escalating inside me. I finished dressing, downed my beer, left the restroom, and said good night to the crew. I exited the building through the back door, got in my car and drove to Larry's

-14-

I arrived at Larry's shortly before 10:00 p.m. The front door was unlocked, so I let myself in and bee-lined upstairs towards Larry's bedroom. I stopped suddenly, like a Michelin tire on a dime, and stood quietly in the hallway outside the door, listening to Darin and Larry talking.

"Man, I'd really appreciate it if you'd run this by Jeannine's for me," Larry asked.

"I don't know," responded Darin

"I'll give you a half if you do this. I'd like to spend some time alone with Louise. You do not have to pick up any money, Jeannine is going to pay me later. "

"O.K., but you'll owe me."

"Thanks, dude," Larry said.

I tapped on the door before I entered the room. Larry sat near the table where he was carefully weighing out a quarter ounce. Darin sat on the bed next to him waiting.

"Hey guys, what's up?"

"Not much. Come on in and have seat. I'm almost finished here," Larry stated, "If you'd like a beer, there are some in the fridge downstairs."

"Sounds great. Do either of you need one?

In unison they said, "yes."

By the time I returned to the room from getting three beers, Larry had put away the scale and was drawing three lines.

Enthusiastically I inhaled my poison and loved every burn and taste as it worked its way into my system. Darin finished his and left to do the favor for Larry. We followed him outside to have a smoke. Darin walked to his car that was parked next door where he lived with his parents, and vanished into the night.

I inhaled deeply. The smoke filled my lungs. The brisk air touched my exposed skin and felt invigorating. Larry's arm encircled my waist. He drew me towards him and I let the cigarette fall from my hand. He pressed his body against mine and tilted his head to kiss me. My head was whirling. My knees became weak. My heart raced. The kiss was deep and passionate.

"What do you say we continue this inside." he murmured, as he swiftly led me through the door and locked it behind me.

"I want to ensure we have absolutely no interruptions for the next twelve hours, at least. All right by you?" he teased

" I cannot think of a place I'd rather be right this minute than in your arms," I said.

My feet left the ground as he held me suspended in his arms. His lips pressed against mine. The temperature was rising. Moisture was beginning to build between my thighs. I wrapped my legs around his waist, my arms braced around his neck. He carried me upstairs, never wavering his hold. He was strong and agile, yet gently placed me on his bed. The mischievous look that had shimmered in his eyes transformed into a gaze of pure animalistic desire. Without haste, but not without thought, he removed my jeans. I felt his finger slip inside me. Skillfully, he moved it along an area on my G-spot. I watched with eager eyes. Soon his face was no longer in my line of vision. I could only see the soft blond hair that covered the back of his head. The flickering motion of his tongue caused my body to involuntarily arch and spasm with pleasure. I closed my eyes, completely enraptured. I was unaware of my screams. He had managed to slip his clothes off at some point while he was seducing me. He slipped my blouse over my head and expertly removed my bra. With the slightest of touch and he spread my legs apart and entered me. The warm, softness of my inner flesh welcomed him inside. In unison, our bodies rose and fell. We made love every few hours for the next twenty-four hours with cat naps in between sessions, only separating for absolute necessities.

Larry left Darin to handle all the business transactions for the thirty-six hours we were together.

By Monday morning, when it was time for me to return home to get ready for my double shift at the Riverside restaurant, every muscle in my body had been worked to its extreme. I was sore, but at the same time amazingly happy. I had a new love in my life. It was the external pleasures of the world that filled the emptiness within me. For awhile, I would feel whole and the hollow feeling I experienced when I was single temporarily disappeared.

-15-

The weeks to follow consisted of Larry and I becoming deeply involved on both an emotional and physical level. I was becoming increasingly more intrigued by the danger of his chosen profession. He shared that part of his life with me in depth. He would take me to his supplier's house and on deliveries with him. The high risk life style of a drug dealer captivated me.

One evening while I was at Larry's house, Rick called. They made arrangements to meet at Michael J's in Ontario near the airport at 9:00 p.m. that evening. Larry drove the Camaro that evening and I accompanied him. We met Rick and his date in the parking lot of the restaurant. Rick was quickly becoming Larry's closest friend and would later be my saving grace. He was a jovial man, tall and of a medium build. His hair was graying, and styled in a seventies shag cut that fell just above his shoulders. His face was partially hidden by the full beard and mustache he wore. A warm inviting smile formed on his lips that would put a raging bull at ease. His eyes, the color of clear blue Caribbean seas, sparkled as if the sun shone directly from inside his soul. Dressed in his latest thrift store purchase, he was a man to be both feared and loved by those who knew him. After hugs and introductions, we walked inside to grab a bite to eat.

"Four, smoking, please," Rick told the hostess.

We were seated at a booth near the window looking out towards the parking lot. The hostess handed each of us a menu and disappeared.

"Did you bring the stuff?" Larry whispered to Rick.

Larry's supply had recently been doubled, in order to keep the business meetings to a once a week occurrence, in hopes of reducing the risk factor of getting busted.

"Don't worry about it. Don't I always take care of you ? Just figure out what you are going to order. It's on me," Rick replied peeking his head over the menu.

Halfway into our meals, Rick's date announced, "I have to go to the bathroom. Louise, why don't you join me?"

"That's O.K. I don't have to go, but thanks for asking," I said, shoving a bite of hash browns into my mouth.

"Louise, you should join her," Rick insisted.

"O.K." I rarely questioned Rick. I slid out of the booth and followed her into the restroom.

She walked directly into a stall and asked to see my purse. I reached over the door and handed it to her, not knowing why. She exited the stall and returned my purse. "It's inside," she stated as she left the bathroom.

"What's inside?" I asked myself out loud. I opened my bag and found a ball of foil the size of a baseball in the bottom. I took it out to look inside.

I walked back to the table with an expression of surprise and disbelief on my face. I sat next to Larry without saying a word.

"Sorry, I didn't warn you first," Rick said, through a mouthful of eggs.

"Uhhhh, that's O.K." I said, unable to mask my discomfort of what had transpired in the bathroom, but able to hold my tongue for the moment.

We finished our meals, said our good-byes and headed our separate ways.

Once inside the Camaro, I let Larry know how angry I was.

"How could you put me in that kind of situation without warning? What if someone had walked in when I had the stuff out? Didn't you think about that? I don't like being put in situations of danger or of getting busted when you could have let me know I was the one making the pick up!" With that said, the ride home was relatively silent.

Once we got inside the house, we did a line and I forgave Larry for his inconsiderateness and careless behavior. As always, I shoved the emotions a bit deeper to make room for some more I did not want to address at that moment.

Larry and Jan inherited a home when their mother died. The house was sitting vacant at the time. Larry talked about moving there often. He even suggested that we live there together.

I did not allow my intrigue and love for Larry to interfere with my studies or work, yet. Every ounce of air I breathed I thought of him, with every heart beat I desired him. It was a euphoric state of mind I remained in until one day, during the first week of March.

-16-

It had been almost a week since I had heard from Larry. I was becoming increasingly alarmed with each passing day that there was no communication between us. My birthday passed with no recognition from Larry. I tried continuously to telephone him and Darin, but received no response. He had closed the door on my heart, and I had missed the good-bye.

Desperate and lonely, I drove to Larry's house. There was no one home. It dawned on me that maybe he was down the street at the house his mother had left him. I recalled a conversation we had that he was seriously considering moving into that house. The house that he lived in was the one his mother, stepfather and he had shared. He had grown up there. The memories inside those walls were becoming torturous. Maybe he had finally decided to let go of his mom and use his inheritance.

The house was located at the end of the cul-de-sac on the same street. It was an average two story colonial home. The floor plan was similar to his mother's house. Larry had taken me there once. I returned to my car and drove over there. I parked along the curb. I could see light seeping through the gaps between the garage door and the wall. I walked to the front door and rang the doorbell. No answer. I persisted. I knew he was inside, I had heard his voice. Although it was barely audible above the music, it was definitely him. The door finally creaked open. The door shielded a good portion of his body as he peered his head around it. His eyes were sunken in and a vacancy sign flashed from the depths of his soul. The flesh on his face pulled tight against his skull.

"Larry it's me, Louise. I have been concerned about you. You have not returned any of my phone calls. May I come in so we can talk?"

"I didn't ask you to come here. What are you doing here? I don't want to see you anymore," he hissed.

It dawned on me pleading was not going to get me inside. I had to change my mind set from the wounded female to a buyer.

"Larry, please let me in. I want to talk business. Do you have anything?"

He nodded and reluctantly stepped away from the entrance to let me pass. I knew he would not pass up the opportunity to make some money. His jeans hung loosely on his body and his rib cage protruded over his abdomen. His hands shook slightly. His eyes darted wildly around the room, as if searching for someone or something else that may have entered his domain with me.

"O.K. what do you want?" he asked as he closed the door behind me

"Uh, a sixteenth, but I only have fifty dollars. I can I pay you the rest in a couple of days." If he agreed, that would enable to see him again. The circumstances were not what I would have preferred, but that didn't matter.

"O.K., but you'd better have the money in two days."

He walked towards the garage. I followed him. Darin was in there and he appeared to be doing some type of mechanical work on Larry's truck. He stopped momentarily to say hello. He had the same waif-like, wild-eyed look as Larry. They were both obviously suffering from sleep deprivation and lack of nutrition.

"When was the last time you two decided to sleep?" I asked.

With a smirk of pride on his lips, Darin said " Oh, about twelve days ago." With that, he returned to what he was doing.

Larry was sitting at metal desk that was placed in the corner of the garage. In front of him was a derringer scale and a baggy of meth. He weighed the sixteenth in silence, then handed it to me. I withdrew the fifty dollars from my purse and placed it on the desk.

He stood from the chair. "You have to go now. I'll walk you to the door," he said.

"But, but" I stammered as he grabbed my arm and led me back through the kitchen to the foyer. I could hear Darin yell bye.

"What are you doing staying up for so many days? That is crazy. You need to take better care of yourself."

"I have to see who the weak ones are. I have to break them. I have to find out who will break under the pressure. Fifteen days," he rattled.

"You're not making any sense. You're suffering from delusional paranoia caused from lack of sleep. You have to get some sleep," I urged.

"You don't belong here. Get out!" He had opened the front door and forcefully guided me through it.

The door slammed behind me. I stood in the dark on the porch, stunned by what I had just seen. I asked myself how the relationship had gone from bliss to total nothingness. Tears began to stream down my face as I looked over my shoulder to the house. Devastated, I walked to my car and left.

-17-

I sat isolated in my room at the apartment. Me and my drugs. The "pink" took away some of the emptiness I was experiencing from being forced out of Larry's house and life so abruptly. How would I find my way back into his arms? Into his life? Well at least I'd see him in a couple of days. Maybe the relationship would resume as quickly as it had dissolved. Time would tell.

For the next twenty four hours I pondered these questions and sought solutions in my mind. I had none, other than I could keep the connection with Larry as my supplier. That would have to be enough. My mind was worked, my body exhausted. I drifted off to sleep a day later.

Jolting up in bed, my brow was dripping with sweat, my lips were parted, my voice letting out a scream. I looked wildly around my room. I realized I was at home, in my room. I was safe. I had nothing to fear at this moment. I lay back down and drifted back to sleep with no further reoccurrence of dreams.

-18-

I awoke the following morning to my radio alarm playing "Purple Haze" in my ears. I had slept for ten hours, but still felt groggy. I had missed one night of rest and gone two days without food. My body and mind rebelled against the neglect. Stiff and sore, I rose from my bed and went to the shower. The hot water pounding on my back eased my muscles slightly. A cup of coffee, muffin and cigarette would take care of the rest. I stepped out of the shower and toweled off before rubbing my skin down with jasmine oil to moisten it. Dressed in a black Nike sweat outfit, the dampness of my hair soaked into the Nike wind breaker. I gathered my books, uniform for work, purse and went to the kitchen and made myself a cup of coffee. I added two heaping spoonfuls of non dairy creamer and was ready to go.

I drove to the college campus. I tried to stay focused on the road as I was driving, but images of Larry kept invading my mind. I arrived on campus at 7:45 a.m., just in time for my first class. Throughout the day my thoughts would wander back to the last time I had seen Larry two days ago. My professors noticed I was distracted during classes. I'd be called on to answer a question, but I was oblivious to the topic. My response was always the same, "Sorry, what was the question?" I finished my classes that day without retaining any information from my lectures. "Thank God for tape recorders," I said to myself as headed to my car to go to work. I had to get it together before I started my shift or it could be disastrous. I managed to collect myself on the drive down the 215 freeway from San Bernardino to Riverside.

My shift flew by that night. I finished my side work around ten. I sat at the bar and had a cocktail with two of my co-workers before making the journey to Larry's to pay him the forty bucks I owed him. I said good night and left the restaurant around 10:30.

-19-

I headed west on the 60 freeway and made my way to the 57 southbound. In a matter of minutes I would be at Larry's. Still dressed in khaki shorts, a pink T-shirt and tennis shoes from work, I walked to the front door and rang the bell.

I looked up into the night sky. There was no moon tonight and the stars were shrouded in a cloud cover. The air was brisk, but comfortable. Concern was sprouting up inside me when no one answered the door. The difference between tonight and two nights hence was the complete darkness that filled the night and the air of death.

Darin answered the door after about ten minutes of insistent ringing. He looked more haggard and withdrawn than he did two days ago. I guess that was to be expected from their no sleep marathon.

"What are you doing here?" he asked.

"I brought the money I owe Larry. Where is he?"

"He doesn't want to see you. You can give the money to me," he said.

"But I want to see him. If he wants his money he will have to collect it. Is he all right?"

Having heard the conversation Larry appeared at the door. A gasp of horror escaped my lips. He looked like a zombie. His skin was ghostly white, his eyes sunk deep into his skull, revealing zero life inside. His body trembled slightly. His voice was sullen and low when he spoke.

"Come in, but only long enough to pay me," he said.

I stepped into the foyer. Darin closed the door behind me. Too stunned to speak, I groped in my purse for the forty dollars. I felt my fingertips come in contact with the cash and withdrew it from my purse. I handed it to Larry. He counted it, told me to get out and walked away. I looked helplessly at Darin. He just shrugged his shoulders and opened the door. Without a word exchanged, I left quietly.

-20-

I returned home that evening feeling sad and confused. I did not understand what had happened to Larry and to our relationship. I felt helpless, but I still had a small amount of hope that things would work out once he came down from his high. That is, if he didn't die first. I needed to talk to someone, who had a connection to Larry. I called Johnny, his cousin.

"Hello?" a male voice greeted on the other end.

"Hi, Johnny?" I said, as I made myself comfortable on my bed. I removed the phone from the table next to the bed and set it on the mattress. I leaned against the pillows padding the back frame. My legs were stretched out in front of me, dangling off the edge.

"Yeah, this is he. Who is this?"

"Hey, it's Louise. What are you up to?"

"I'm getting ready to crash. I have to work early tomorrow. So what do I owe the pleasure of this call?"

I told him briefly about the episode with Larry and the fact that we were no longer dating. My voice betrayed my feelings of loss, frustration and disappointment. I tried to keep the tears from coming, but that turned out to be an impossible task.

"What do you want with that loser, anyway? You're far to good to be involved with him. You should be dating me," he said, somewhat in jest, but with a hint of truth behind his words.

He managed to bring a chuckle to my lips, for that I was grateful. I avoided his remark about dating because I was simply not interested. Although, Larry was his cousin, he felt no loyalty towards him. Theirs was a relationship of convenience and kinship, not necessarily friendship. Having the opportunity to be a part of Johnny's life would possibly bring me back into Larry's life, if I played my cards right.

"What do you say we do something sometime? Me and my roomies usually go dancing at least one night a week. Why don't you join us? We'll dance," I asked.

"That might be a possibility. Why don't you give me call in the next couple of weeks and I'll let you know for sure then. Hey, chin up. You really are better off without him. I'm not just saying that because I want to take you out. I'll talk to you later," he said.

"O.K. bye," I said.

I hung up the phone and lay silently in the dark, unable to sleep, I made another call.

"Hello," a groggy male voice answered.

"Hi, Mitch, it's me. Sorry to wake you, but I need to talk, if that 's all right." He was an extremely early riser. That was one of the many differences between us. He would be leaving for work at 5:00 a.m. while I'd just be entering my deepest sleep pattern. While I found my solace in the dark, he found his in light.

"What is up? Is something wrong?" I could hear the movement of waterbed mattress. He was moving around on the bed as he made himself comfortable.

"I was just feeling sad. Larry doesn't want to see me anymore, but the thing is, I am worried about him. I went by there to pay him some money I owed him and he'd been up for almost two weeks straight. He looked like he had one foot in his grave. Mitch, are you still with me?" I could tell he was drifting off. I asked myself why I had bothered to call him, it was because I trusted him and felt safe talking to him. He still was my best friend, even though I had left the marriage.

As I was answering my own questions in my thoughts, I heard him say, "Yeah, I am still here. You know it's his choice if he wants to kill himself. There is nothing you can do. I'm having a difficult time being sympathetic, considering my feelings for you and our past. You know I care about you deeply, but I don't know what you want from me, Louise. I don't like him, and I have never led you to believe otherwise. He is only good for one thing as far as I am concerned. I don't need to elaborate any further. What do you want from me?" There was an impatient edge to his voice.

"Mitch, just be my friend. That is all I want from you," I said softly, as I rolled over onto my right side, still cradling the phone to my left ear.

"You have that. What do you say we go out and do something next week. I'll come down to your apartment and can we go from there."

"I'd like that very much. Let's go Saturday and since it's your birthday I'll take you out. Whatever you want to do, O.K.? Oh, and thanks for being there for me. I really appreciate it. I'll call you next week. Bye." With that I hung up the phone. The loneliness I had been feeling began to dissipate. Mitch always had the ability to help me put things in perspective. I lay on my back, hands folded across my chest in the darkness, and closed my eyes.

-21-

The wet weather continued for most of the week. It suited my spirit. Although my heart held on to feelings for Larry with restraints that would hold a bear, my mind buried the files in the archives of its basement. Melancholy and sad, I went to work, turning on the charm when I needed to, but inside was nothing but bleakness. I went to school, turned my assignments in on time, took my exams, and spoke to no one unless absolutely necessary. The sun was beginning to break through the cloud covered sky by Thursday. The gloom and doom within me melted with the shining of the sun, like the snow covered mountains which began to defrost with the first warm day after a bitter winter. By Friday, the sky had turned blue.

Sitting in the office at the Whole Enchilada, phone in my right hand, cigarette in my left, I stared absently at the clock on the shelf over my head as Mitch chattered about tomorrow's plans. He would meet me at my apartment around nine, then we would go to the Tree House for cocktails and dancing.

Mitch was never a dancer, but he knew that when I was on the dance floor, only the moment and the movement existed for me. The only time in the last seven years I had persuaded Mitch to dance with me was at a family birthday party. We had far too much to drink that night. I grabbed his hand, pulled him on to the dance floor and wrapped his arms around my waist. We swayed rhythmically to the seduction of music. That would be the one and only time we would ever dance together. On the way home that evening, we ended up in the ice plant on the side of the freeway. Mitch had missed the exit and made a sharp right towards the off ramp, but there was a divider he did not see. The truck lurched over the concrete, cleared the lane, and landed on the shoulder, which was covered in this green sticky vegetation, iceplant.

Snapped out of my revere, I acknowledged the plans with an "uh-huh"

"Can you see if you can get a half gram for us tomorrow?" he asked.

"Sure, I'll call Darin. Do you want to get some dinner before we go to the bar?

"Let's play that by ear. I'll see you tomorrow."

A dial tone hummed in my ear for a moment before I realized Mitch had hung up. I twirled around in the office chair as I let my thoughts continue to drift on tomorrow's date with my soon to be ex husband.

-22-

The door bell rang at 9:15 p.m. Saturday night. Dressed and ready to spend the evening with Mitch I answered the door. Mitch stood before me clad in a pair of gray pleated cotton Dockers, a cotton striped purple and gray button front shirt. I had purchased the clothes he wore this evening shortly before our separation, although I'd been unable to convince him to wear it at the time. The top three buttons were undone, revealing the curly blond hair that covered his chest. I used to love to run my fingers across his chest, to feel the soft texture of the hairs brushing against my appendages. A gold herringbone chain hung just below his collar bone an eagle made of gold wings spread with a diamond positioned at wing tip. His lightly, tanned skin enhanced the crystal blue of his eyes. His curly blonde hair was cut short above the ears and fell a fraction above his shoulders. His smile was gentle, kind and warm, his upper lip hidden by a thick light colored mustache. His teeth were colored ever so slightly from nicotine and caffeine, but each was perfectly aligned.

"Come in, come in," I gestured with a sweep of my hand. I stepped away from the entrance. "How's the birthday boy? You look great. I have something for you. Follow me." I led him to my bedroom and said, "Have a seat I'll just be a minute." He moved towards the bed and sat down. I rummaged in my purse for a moment and pulled out a baggy. "Here we are." Holding it up to show Mitch, I asked, "Would you like one now?"

"I haven't eaten today. Let's grab a burger at Carl's then do one," he suggested as he glanced around the room.

"O.K. let's go." I put the baggy in the side compartment of my purse and threw the strap over my shoulder.

I followed behind Mitch as we left the apartment and walked to the car port. "Why don't you drive?" I said as I tossed him the keys to the Camaro. Forever the gentleman, Mitch opened the passenger door for me and I slid into the bucket seat. I leaned over to the driver's door and unlocked it. Mitch slipped behind the wheel and placed the key in the ignition. I leaned over and gently kissed his cheek. "Thanks for coming over tonight. I'm really looking forward to this evening." He turned to face me, and our eyes held one another for a moment. Years of familiarity and friendship filled my heart.

"So am I," The Camaro lurched forward and we were on our way to Diamond Bar.

First we stopped at Carl Junior and each ordered a Happy Star and small fries. We sat in the parking lot eating and talking about nothing in particular. We finished our food, left Carl's and headed towards the Tree House night club. We passed the club and turned into a residential area nearby. Mitch switched off the lights and killed the engine.

I grabbed the baggy from my purse, a credit card, and a tape case from floorboard and chopped us each a monster line. "You first, birthday boy." He already had a billed rolled in his hand, waiting. The only noise inside the car was the sound of Mitch's deep inhale. I followed, then placed the baggy in the center console along with the tape case. "I am ready to have some fun, how about you?" I asked as my eyes were watering and my nostrils burning.

We drove back to the bar, parked the car and went inside. There were many familiar faces scattered throughout the two levels of the club. We strolled over to the downstairs bar and ordered a couple of Heinekens. We walked upstairs to a empty pool table and placed three quarters in the slots and waited for the balls to drop out. Sounds of the Doors boomed in the back ground, performed by a local night club band. I leaned over the railing. The dance floor was semi-full, and singles and couples alike buzzed around the bar greeting people they knew. The dim lighting of the bar made it difficult for me to distinguish the faces of those below, but I could see the white glow of teeth under the black lights when they smiled. Absorbed in the movements of strangers, I had tuned out all else.

"Hey," Mitch said, as he tapped me on the shoulder, bringing me back to that moment. "I've been calling your name. Where were you? The balls are racked and ready. Do you still want to play?"

"Of course. I was just thinking about the first time you asked me out. Do you realize that was over seven years ago? Who ever would have believed that we would be standing here right now. Anyway, sorry I drifted off." I threw my arms around his neck and pulled him close. "Let's play."

It turned out to be an evening of reminiscing with friends and laughter filled the conversations. Mitch played pool, and feeling the adrenaline pumping, I had to dance. I left Mitch and headed down the stairs to the dance floor. I moved around the floor, dancing by myself until some familiar faces joined me. After a number songs, I returned upstairs. Twice during the evening we slipped away to continue the rush. The evening was wrapping up. We said good bye to our friends and left.

In the car heading back to the apartment, music played softly on the radio. I leaned over to Mitch and rested my head on his shoulder as he drove. "Would like to stay at the apartment tonight? I don't want you to drive all the way at this time of the morning."

"That would be a good idea. Thanks. I had a good time tonight," he said, keeping his eyes on the road ahead.

We arrived back the apartment around 2:00 a.m. We went directly to the bedroom. "Would you like another line?" I asked.

"Sure, but just a small one" he said, as he made himself comfortable on the bed.

I handed him the baggy and utensils. "You go head and draw them up. I'm going to slip into something more comfortable and wash my face."

I could hear the tapping of the plastic credit card against mirror as I removed my clothing and wrapped myself in cotton blend, thigh length robe. I walked over to the night stand, picked up the mirror and cleaned it spotless.

Mitch was lying on the bed on his back, arms crossed under his head, by the time I did my line. He was now the one lost in thought, staring up at the ceiling, looking at nothing that existed in that room. I sat down on the edge of the bed and leaned over him, with a hand positioned on each side of his body. "Hey are you O.K.? You seem a bit distracted and melancholy." I saw pain and sadness in his eyes when he stared back at me.

Softly, he said "I was just thinking about us. The times we shared. After seven years together most of the memories I recall are remembered with fondness and love. That is, when they don't make me sad. There are moments when I miss you, your company. The laughter and even the tears. I sit down for dinner and look at the seat besides me and it's empty. Both the seat and my soul at that moment. I know that you have to do what you have to do, even though I don't understand why. I only need to accept it and move on, but that is not always easy." His eyes filled with tears as he spoke from his heart. Mitch was never much for idle chit chat, so when he spoke I listened.

I was wrapped in an enigma of confusion and inability to understand a relationship that had gone awry and oblivious to the dysfunction inside his cocoon. His armor had always kept him untainted from loss of a love. For if he never loved, he never had to mend his heart. He did not realize what he gave up for his shield of protection until the day it was removed, for if he never gave love, he would never receive love.

"Mitch, I wish I could have been the wife you deserved. If I could, I would replace all your sadness and loneliness with joy and love. You deserve to have someone in your life that can return the love that you give and appreciate your warmth, loyalty and kindness. I am not capable of that at this point in my life. I am truly sorry I hurt you. You've been my best friend, my lover and my confidant for one third of my life. I will always have a special place in my heart for you. We've both grown, but our roads are no longer parallel. We came to a fork, and the path was only wide enough for one soldier. It is a journey I must do alone. I know you do not understand this right now, but in time, we will heal and you'll forget about me. I only hope that someday you can forgive me. Mitch, I do love you, but that would have never been enough." He looked into my eyes, listening and trying to grasp the meaning of my words. Words that flooded from my lips, words that I did not even understand. I felt the warmth of a tear trickle down my cheek as I spoke. "Will you hold me?" He nodded his head. I stretched my body next to his, lying on my side. I rested my head on his chest and placed my arm over his body. He was still fully clothed with the exception of his shoes. He wrapped his arm around me. I knew in my heart this would be the last time we would hold each other. For that I silently wept. I drifted in and out of sleep for the next few hours. Even the drugs were not able to dispel the sorrow and loss I felt in his arms, nor did they keep rest from me tonight.

I felt Mitch move from under me and get off the bed. I rolled over and glanced at the clock. It read 6:30 a.m. "Where are you going?" I asked, " It's early."

"I have to go. Thanks again for everything," he said.

I could tell he had not slept. "Are you sure you're all right to drive?

"Yeah, I'm fine. I'll talk to you later."

"Can you do me a favor then? Please. When you get home call and let me know you made it safely. You can just leave a message on the machine."

"Sure." He bent down, kissed me on the cheek and left.

The winter quarter was winding down. The energy floating in the air on campus was stressed. Students opened books for last minute cramming in a vain attempt to absorb any information they may not have absorbed. I was among the crammers.

As always, finals came and went with huge sighs of relief to be out for spring break. The air seemed to become lighter. Smiles replaced the quizzical looks of tension on the faces of the students.

I left campus after my last final, ready for a little fun. My mind was already in party mode.

I had taken the evening off work with the intention of going dancing at the Tree House. I dressed in my usual risqué attire for night clubbing. I went alone with the forethought of maybe meeting someone. It had been over a month since Larry and I had any sexual contact. I was longing to feel the flesh of a man next to me.

I arrived at the Tree House around 10:00 that evening and headed straight for the bar. After I slammed a watermelon shooter and drank a bay breeze I was ready to mingle. I looked around the lower level to see if there was anyone I knew. On the far side of the room I spotted Darin with a couple of guys. I immediately strolled over to their table.

"Hey, what's up?" I asked. Salacious thoughts entered my mind when Darin stood and tenderly hugged me. With a couple cocktails in my system, sexual desire overrode everything.

Our eyes locked and held the gaze until Darin turned his head to introduce me to his friends. He was clad in a pair of blue jeans that were faded in just the right spots drawing my attention to that particular area of his body. A white T-shirt pressed against his torso, outlining every muscle. A black leather jacket was tossed over the stall next to him.

"Why don't you join us?" Darin invited

"Sure," I replied as I moved the jacket and sat on the seat next to Darin.

We talked and laughed. We got caught up on each other's lives, since the only contact we'd, had in about five weeks was brief business dealings.

"Let's dance!" I said, excitedly grabbing Darin's hand and pulling him off the stool.

"O.K." he said, showing no resistance to my forcefulness.

The Scorpions' "Send Me An Angel" wailed on the sound system. We swayed to the music with arms wrapped around each other. Our bodies pressed against one another, with sweat seeping through my shirt from the heat of moment.

"Let's get out of here," Darin whispered in my ear.

Without answering in words, I removed myself from his embrace, took his hand and led him out of the club. I followed him in my car to his house. The moisture between my legs was building with anticipation.

We parked in front of his house. I could see Larry's truck in his driveway, but I was too drunk to care if Larry found out about our rendezvous. Darin put his finger to his lips, a motion to quiet my giggles as we walked into his house where he lived with his parents. His room was in the front of the house; once we were inside, we would not disturb his parents in the back of the house. Not one second passed before we were committing pure unadulterated acts. I ran my fingers through his raven colored hair, stopping at the base of the hair line, firmly gripping the underside of his thick hair and gently tugging his back. He ran his hand underneath my skirt, titillating and caressing the area covered by my panties. He pulled my panties to the floor, then lifted my feet to remove them from my body. Ardently, he grabbed my hips, lifting me on to a night table. I swiftly undid his jeans and pushed them down his thighs with my feet. He entered me and thrust in and out. His lips, slippery and wet, remained occupied on my face, my neck, and my lips. Like a starved woman, I devoured him.

The following morning he kissed me.

"Good morning," I said sleepily, "What time is it?"

"Nine o clock," he responded.

"I had better go. Thanks for a wonderful evening. I'll never forget it, but let's just keep it between us," I said, slipping into my clothes.

"Of course, just between friends. I'll see you later."

He walked me to my car and hugged me tightly good-bye.

-24-

I finally decided to call Johnny."Hey, there stranger, sorry I didn't call you sooner. It has been kind of hectic. Between finals and work, that's all I have had time for these last few weeks. I thought I was about to sink for a bit there. Anyway, I finished finals last Thursday. It is time to let loose. Would you like to meet me, Janis and Carol for a drink at Red Onion in La Habra?"

"Sure, I'll bring Al and Jim. What time are you guys going to be there?"

"We'll be there around 9:30, see you then," I said, then hung up the phone.

I could feel myself returning to a normal emotional state. Although I still wasn't giving up on Larry, I decided it was a good idea to step back. I trotted into Janis' room and told her Johnny and some friends would be meeting us tonight. She always was a firm believer of "the more the merrier."

"What are you wearing?" I inquired

"Well, I'll probably wear a pair of black stretch pants, a black top, my black low heeled boots and a black blazer. You know how much I like black," she said giggling.

"I am going to shower and dress. Let's leave about 9:20. O.K."

"O.K."

I showered quickly. It was 8:30 when I stepped from the bathroom. Water dripped slowly down my back and chest from my hair. When the moisture reached my nipples they perked up. I glanced at my nudity in the mirror. I loved to be naked. To feel life, whatever it maybe, against my exposed flesh. I was hornier than a rabbit in heat. " No time to go there," I thought to myself as I squeezed a palm full of jasmine massage oil into hand to rub over my skin.

I removed a cotton kacki mini skirt, white blazer and one inch pumps from the closet. I carefully selected my under garments and a midriff sleeveless floral print red, kacki and white top from the bureau. I slipped on my clothes in order of necessity.

I leaned my upper body towards the mirror while I applied my make up, then dried my hair, ratted the bangs to give them some height, and I was ready to go. I grabbed my wallet and keys then slipped them into my blazer pocket and left my room.

"Hey, you guys ready? It is almost 9:30. Let's go. I'll drive," I yelled

They both stepped into the living room. They were dressed in similar outfits, the only difference was that Carol wore only a colorful brazier under her blazer. They looked beautiful, as always.

Carol was 5'4" a hundred pounds of hard body, with light brown hair all one length that cascaded down her back to her tail bone. Her facial features were sharp and chiseled. Her small round breast filled the cups of her bra nicely. Large brown, oval eyes with lashes that touched the stars were her most alluring asset. She exuded sex.

Janis, the more conservative of the three of us, also stood 5'4. Her bone structure was slightly larger than Carol's, and she was built with a stocky frame. Her hair was naturally black and ringlet curls began at her scalp and continued the full length of her excessively long hair. She wore long bangs covering her forehead. She had almond shaped green eyes with thick black lashes-- cat's eyes. Most of her figure resided in her hips. Her breasts small and dainty, her lips full and lush.

We were definitely ready to prowl tonight.

We left the apartment and arrived at the Red Onion at approximately 9:45. We sauntered inside and made our way to the bar.

"I'd like a Stoli bay breeze," I said turning my head to ask the girls what they would like. "A Coors light and sex on the beach," I ordered from the bartender.

I paid the bartender. I handed Janis her beer and Carol her cocktail. We started wandering through the crowd to see if our friends were there.

I felt a hand encircle my waist from behind, sending me immediately on the defensive. I whirled around hand raised to slap this unwelcome stranger when I met Johnny's laughing eyes. I threw my arm around him and gave him a hug.

"You almost got slapped, mister. I'm glad you could make it. It is good to see you."

"Even if I had gotten slapped it would have been worth it just to see the expression on your face before you realized it was me. I bet you can handle yourself when you need to." He planted a friendly kiss on my cheek, and I lead him and his buddies through the crowd to find the girls.

After introductions we danced, drank and laughed all night. When it came time to leave, I noticed Carol was nowhere to be found.

"Janis, where is Carol? I can't seem to find her."

"Oh, she wasn't feeling to hot so she got a ride home about an hour ago. No worries."

"Let's go, Johnny. Why don't you guys stay at the apartment? I don't think you should be driving all the way home. We just live down the street," I suggested.

"Thanks, Wee'lll doo thatt " Johnny slurred.

Janis, Johnny, Al, Jim and I arrived back to our apartment at 2:15 a.m. Easter morning. We had been out dancing and drinking all night. We allowed the guys to crash at our pad since it was late and they were intoxicated. Johnny and Al slept in my bedroom on the floor, while Jim made his bed in Janis' room. The minute my head hit the pillow, I was fast asleep.

-25-

The sound of a fist crashing against my door jolted me into consciousness.

"Wake up," Carol yelled through the door, "You'll be late for work."

I immediately jumped out of bed, and looked at the clock, which read 7:30 a.m. Thinking it was Monday morning and that I had slept through Easter, I panicked. How could I have slept thirty hours? As I made my way to the door, I tripped over Johnny who still was asleep on my bedroom floor. I opened the door. At that moment I saw Janis peering out her door.

"Happy Easter!" Carol shouted joyously.

In front of each of our doors Carol had placed a large Easter basket filled with various delectable chocolates and a white and pink floppy eared stuffed bunny.

Realizing that I had only slept for five hours and that it was Sunday, not Monday, my panicked feeling completely evaporated and was replaced with elation. I pick up my new stuffed bunny and squeezed it tight. Janis, also very cheerful at the Easter Bunny's arrival, gathered her bunny and followed suit.

"Time for an Easter egg hunt," Carol declared.

With laughter in our hearts and the spirit of the moment in our souls, we woke the guys to include them in our celebration. Like children on their first hunt, we whole-heatedly, scoured the apartment for every last candy filled egg. Carol stood by and hinted towards the direction of the last eggs. Upon finishing our morning endeavor, Janis and I rolled around on the floor with our stuffed bunnies while Carol snapped some pictures.

Easter was Carol's favorite holiday and the only one in which she enjoyed celebrating. It was one of those moments of complete, unexpected joy and fun I will never forget.

Shortly after the celebration, Johnny, Al and Jim headed home.

"Our family is having a get together at the park if you care to come. They rent the park for the day, play games and barbecue. It starts about 2:00 p.m.," Johnny said, before he headed out the door.

"I'll call you later and let you know. Thanks."

Carol, Janis and I threw on some sweats and headed to the IHOP for breakfast. Returning from breakfast, Janis and Carol hopped in the shower to prepare for their day with their families. I, on the other hand, had no plans. I decided to call Johnny.

"Hi, Johnny," I greeted.

"Hey, what's up?" he asked.

"I thought I'd take you up on your invitation."

"Great. Meet me at my house at 1:30 and we'll go to the park from here."

"See you then. Bye," I said.

"Bye."

I showered, dressed in a pair of black shorts, a tank top and tennis shoes. I was ready for a day that had already started out ideal. This would be the most memorable Easter of my life.

I picked Johnny up on time and we headed for a park over on Rosecrantz. The day was warm and the sky radiated a brilliant blue over our heads. I could see the mountains to the north. The peaks were covered in snow. When we arrived, there was about a hundred people gathered and barricades that read "private party." People were drinking beer, feasting, playing volleyball and softball.

I joined right in. I grabbed a bottle of water and headed for the volleyball courts. Volleyball was my favorite sport to play. I waited on the side lines while the game that was in progress finished up. I was invited to join one of the teams for the next match. We played a few games before deciding to take a break and to eat.

"Let the games begin!" Johnny's mom shouted after we ate.

We played a number of different innovative ridiculous games. I participated in most. With each game, the winner or winners received these recycled trophies. The trophies had plastic egg shells strung from the figurine that was positioned at the top. Wrapping ribbon connected the shells to one another with other innovative decorations appropriately placed in between the shells. I had the honor of being on the team that won the human toilet paper roll competition. I laughed my ass off as five of us began wrapping toilet paper around our bodies, careful not to break the thin delicate tissue connection between each member. Five of us stood in a straight line behind one another, the leader would take the end of the roll twirl himself around it twice. Each member would do this then it would be passed back up the line through each member's legs. If the roll separated your team was out.

We finished the games and went back to volleyball. I continued to drink water throughout the day because I knew I had to drive home. The sun was beginning to go down so we wrapped up the game, cleaned up the park and a bunch of us headed to Johnny's.

Shortly after we returned to Johnny's, another guest arrived. I was sitting at the kitchen table sipping on a glass of grapefruit juice visiting with Johnny's mom, Diane. My back faced the front door. I heard the screen door squeak open. I turned to see Larry and Darin stepping into the entry way. Our eyes met. Disbelief was betrayed in Larry's eyes when he saw me. Quickly it turned to anger. The tension began to immediately rise in air. I turned back to Diane and apologized for causing any conflict. Darin and I had not spoken since our lascivious encounter. The discomfort in my gut was not sparked by his presence, but by Larry's.

"Honey, you were invited here. We have enjoyed having you. Larry will get over it. He has always been moody ever since his dad and mom were divorced when he was seven. Then it only escalated with the suicide of his brother and the death of his mom. Besides, he if chooses to allow you to affect his moods or him having good time, that is his choice. You are welcome here. Don't forget that," Johnny's mom said.

"Thanks I appreciate that."

Larry turned right down the hallway with Darin following close behind. They went to the first bedroom on the left where a couple of people were hanging out smoking some grass. I could hear bits and pieces of the conversation when the voices would raise above normal pitch.

"What the hell is she doing here!" Larry shouted.

"I invited her. Besides, I asked you if you wanted to come to the picnic you said - - and I quote 'why the hell would I waste my time playing a bunch of stupid games and hanging out with losers.' I took that to mean you would not be attending," Johnny countered smugly.

"Well, that doesn't matter. She has no right to be here. You are my family! Tell her to leave, right now or I will leave," Larry threatened.

I could here muffled conversation through the closed door, but I was unable to distinguish what was being said after Larry threatened to leave. I waited patiently. I was expecting to be asked to leave the minute the bedroom door opened. What happened next was a welcome and comforting surprise to me. Larry glared at me. Every muscle seemed tense, like a wild beast that just realized another had inhabited his territory, while he was out hunting and he lost the fight to regain possession. He and Darin walked to the front door to leave. Without a word, Larry opened the door and stepped outside. Darin turned to me, winked, and waved good bye. Darin and I remained fast friends now that we shared an intimate secret. Small innuendoes that only made sense to Darin or I were the only things said about that lustful, wonderful night. With a shrug of his shoulders, he stepped out behind Larry.

Johnny came into the kitchen following Larry's abrupt departure. I turned to him. I must have had a look of bewilderment on my face, because Johnny began to laugh.

"Don't look so surprised. You are my guest here. No one, not even my cousin, comes into my house and tells me who belongs here and who doesn't. You are much more fun anyway. Certainly better looking. Now, why don't we play ping pong?"

Johnny did surprise me. I did enjoy hanging out with him and his friends. "O.K. let's play. I'll kick your ass," I replied with a chuckle.

"We'll see about that."

We played ping pong and relaxed until around 10:30 that evening. As I was making my rounds to say good bye, I entered one of the bedrooms. One of the guys had just bought a gram of coke.

"Hey would you like a line before you leave?" he inquired.

I thought about it for a moment before saying yes. The conversation I had in my head prior to saying yes went something like this. "It is late and you're tired this will keep you up just long enough to drive home. You don't want to fall asleep at the wheel, do you?" Accepting a line made perfect sense at the time. I did my line. As I was heading to my car, Johnny and his parents tried to convince me to spend the night and drive home in the morning. I thanked them for their invitation, but graciously declined.

I pulled out of the driveway and immediately spotted a police car on my tail. I quickly searched for my glasses. I had forgotten them at home. A slight panic began to bubble up inside me. I am near-sighted and found my vision impairment was at its worst driving at night. I told myself to remain calm. I hadn't been drinking and the coke hadn't had time to reach my system yet. I kept an eye on the rear view mirror as I turned right onto Rosecrantz.

Behind, I spotted the red light of the police car. Instantly I pulled to the side of the road. The cocaine was rushing through my blood stream, causing my heart to pound heavily in my chest now. I rolled down my window as the officer approached my car.

"Can I see your driver's license," he asked.

As I handed him my license, he asked, " Do you know why I pulled you over?"

"No sir," I responded.

"You made a right hand turn on a red light."

I had been unaware that was illegal on this street. I had missed the sign because I could not see it without my glasses. It was a street where you could make a quick right or a wide right on the other side of an island. I did not know there was an island.

"Have you been drinking?" the officer asked.

"No sir," I responded.

"Do you mind if I search your car," he asked.

"No," I said.

"Please step out of the car," he said, as he opened the door and directed me towards the curb.

I stepped out of the car. The night air was chilly on my bare skin. I walked over to the sidewalk, sat on the curb, pulled my knees to my chest, wrapped my arms around my legs and waited. The officer noticed that I was not dressed for the cool evening air and asked if I would like to sit in the car and wait while he finished. The only thought that went through my mind was if I sat inside that police car I was never getting out.

"No, thank you," I replied, rocking back and forth in hopes removing the external chill.

"Really, it's O.K. I'm not going to arrest you," he said, appearing sympathetic to my fear.

"I'm fine. Thanks."

Minutes before he finished the search of my car, an undercover narc pulled up behind the police car. The narc stepped out of his car and walked directly towards me. He was dressed in slacks and a Polo shirt.

"Can you please stand?" he asked, although it was an order shaped in the form of a question. Without hesitation, I stood up.

Once I was standing up, he flashed his light directly into my eyes. I squinted in response to the bright light.

"Have been using any amphetamines? Your pupils are dilated," he said.

"Excuse me, what?" I asked, with shock in my voice.

"Uppers, cocaine, crystal," he said, clarifying the question.

I was becoming increasingly more alarmed at the narc's line of questioning. Unnerved, I told the officer I had tried coke three nights ago at a bar for the first time. They tried to extract specifics who, what, where. I told him I didn't know, it was just some guys at a bar in Orange county.

The cops performed a couple of different sobriety tests on me. I passed the drunk test, but not the twelve second speed test. The next thing I heard was "Place your hands behind your back, you are being arrested for suspicion of driving under the influence of narcotics." The metal cuffs felt like ice against my skin as the officer placed them around my wrists. Tears began streaming down my face. My mind was riddled with confusion as I was placed gently in the back seat of the black and white.

As we drove to the station, the officer apologized profusely for the turn of events. That did not alleviate any of my fear.

"You were in the wrong place at the wrong time." he said repeatedly. "I'm sorry, but was it worth it? Drugs are never worth the consequences they invoke."

I sat speechless and sobbing in the back seat. When we arrived at the Norwalk sheriff station, the officer removed the cuffs and began the booking process. My tears subsided for awhile. The officer proceeded to ask me what I had been doing this evening and if there was any drinking and drugging going on, but I stood by my original lie.

"Would you submit to a urine test?" he asked.

"What happens if I say no?" I responded

"Well, you will be held at least seventy-two hours, and in essence, become guilty by unwillingness to cooperate," he stated sternly and effectively.

I bought it hook, line, and sinker. "O.K. I'll agree to take the test," I said.

A large black woman entered the booking room to oversee that I take a urine test, and she confiscated my shoelaces and belt. The removal of these items sent me into a hysterical crying fit. I did not comprehend why she took these items. All I knew was that I felt violated. The fear made me unable to pee for an hour and half. The officers waited patiently. Finally the booking process was finished and I was taken to a holding cell where I was allowed to make one phone call before they would take me down to the jail.

I called Johnny. The sobbing made it difficult for me talk.

"They took my shoe laces and belt, why?" I sobbed.

"They take anything that a person possibly could harm themselves or others with," he told me.

"What harm could a pair of shoe strings cause?" I naively asked.

"They don't want you hanging yourself," he said.

When I realized the implication of that statement I wailed in the phone, "I want my shoe strings back, I would rather be dead than be here."

"You'll be fine. When they take you to your cell, stop crying and go to sleep. They can only hold you for 72 hours."

The thought of spending even one night in jail sent me into a suicidal rage. I talked to Johnny for almost two hours before the officer motioned for me to hang up.

"Whatever you do, when you get to the cell, don't act like a blubbering child. Call me when they release you. I will pick up your car and bring it to my house. Don't worry, you'll be fine," he said, reassuringly.

I hung up the phone and was immediately escorted to the jail. The jailer led me down a brightly lit corridor. A barred door slid open that led to the individual cells. There were only two cells in this particular hall. I was placed in the one furthest away from the entrance. The bars slamming behind me summoned a sudden reserve and fear within me. I immediately plugged up the well of tears and climbed onto the top bunk. I shared the cell with two other women. I closed my eyes and slept until breakfast was served. Breakfast consisted of watery kool-aid and some dry toast. I thought bread and water was just something I had seen on TV.

The cell doors were opened within the corridor. There was a community shower, toilet and wash basin located at the end of the corridor. I stepped out of the box I had been put in and sat on the cold cement floor of the other cell. Although I said nothing, I listened to the stories that had brought my present roommates together. About 10:00 a.m. we were all herded to the holding cell and where we could each make a phone call. As I waited for my turn, I heard my name being called by the officer positioned outside the cell.

"Louise Tote, will you please come with me," he said.

I stepped up to the bars and the officer cracked it open, grabbed my arm and pulled me out. He quickly locked the door behind me. Confused and tired, I stood still waiting to find out why I had been summoned.

"You have been released on O.R. Here are your personal effects. Your court date is April 12. You are free to go."

Taking the envelope with my things and the paper work, I walked outside the station. I found a phone nearby and called Johnny to pick me up. Johnny arrived within fifteen minutes of my call. He took me to his house to get my car. I called work from Johnny's and explained I had gotten arrested and would not be in for my first shift, but I would return to work that evening. Then I drove back to my apartment.

27

That evening, I arrived for my Monday night cocktail shift. Overjoyed by my quick release, I managed to put on my happy face for the evening. Upon arrival, the manager pulled me aside to find out the details of my absence.

"So what happened?" Joe, the manager, asked.

Looking him directly in the eyes I told him "I had been drinking, but I was pulled over for a traffic violation. At which time the officer smelled alcohol on my breath and proceeded to arrest me for driving under the influence." I told him the truth about the remainder of the incident. I intentionally did not share with him the fact that it was a drug related charge. I knew that would be unacceptable. He bought my lie, and that was the story I stuck to with most of my coworkers and family.

The night passed quickly. I enjoyed working this shift. Spirits were usually high.

I left work and headed straight for home, exhausted from little solid sleep the night before. I slept like a rock that evening.

28

I returned to my routine the following day of school and work, but the charges weighed heavy on my mind. I was completely ignorant on how to approach my defense. I also had no means for an attorney at that time. I sought the only people I knew that could advise me on the necessary steps to take that would induce minimal punishment.

After I finished my classes for the day, I went directly to work and placed a phone call to Karen and Arron. I knew they both had the day off. My only hope was that they would be home.

Karen answered the phone in her usual cheerful voice.

"Hey, honey, it's Louise. Are you and Arron going to be home this evening around 9:00, 9:30? If so, I really need to stop by and talk to you two." I glanced around the hostess station of the restaurant as I spoke to her.

"Yeah, we'll be here. Is everything all right?" she asked with concern in her voice.

Turning my back to the hostess desk, I said, "Yes and no, but not to worry. I'll tell you about it tonight when I see you. I'll talk to you later. Bye." I hung up the pay phone, feeling simultaneously relieved and afraid about talking to them about my situation. In order to get any helpful, advice I had to be completely honest with about the charges.

Karen had become one of my dearest and closest friends over the past few of years. She was aware of my most of my indiscretions, but not my drug use. She was discerning, and I knew I could trust her with a secret.

I met Karen almost three years prior when I came in to interview at El Gato Gordo. Her first impression of me was that I was a bitch, but she was given the task of training me. She found that although her first impression was not necessarily inaccurate, there were many more qualities upon which we could build a solid, long lasting friendship. She took the first step to opening the door. She invited me water skiing at Lake Perris. That was the beginning of a life long friendship. When we would go places together, more often than not, people asked if we were sisters sometimes even twins. Although she was about three inches shorter than me, our facial features and builds were very similar. It was definitely the eyes. Karen eyes were beautiful smoky brown pools. She could work wonders batting her eyes when she wanted to. Her eyes were a much lighter shade than mine, but nonetheless both our most alluring feature.

Arron, was a police officer, and Karen's boyfriend. I needed his expertise on how to approach my case before I had to stand before the judge.

When my shift was over I went directly to Arron's house, which was about ten minutes from the restaurant. I arrived. Karen welcomed me in with a hug.

"So what's up?" she inquired

"Well, Sunday night I was arrested for driving and being under the influence of narcotics." Quickly and honestly I explained the circumstances of the event to both Karen and Arron. Once I finished my tale I showed Arron the ticket which included a list of charges.

"I didn't know you used cocaine," she said with surprise in her voice.

"Once in awhile," I lied

"First, ask for a public defender. Plead not guilty to the charge of driving under the influence. No contest to under the influence, because if you are found guilty of the first crime your license will be suspended for six months and a large fine will be attached. Most likely, it will be dropped since this is your first offense. On the second charge you will still receive a fine, plus some type of rehabilitation program and probation." he suggested after reading the ticket.

We visited for a bit longer, I thanked them for their help and headed home.

-29-

With a strategy in mind and some insight into the justice procedures, I was able to put the arrest out of my thoughts temporarily and concentrate on school and work during the following week.

About a week or so after the arrest I received a phone call from Larry, much to my astonishment. I had not heard from or seen him since Easter Sunday. I opted not to return his call until the following day due to exhaustion, both mental and physical, from the hectic week. I made note of the calls I needed to return, then readied myself for sleep.

I found myself in a haze pinching my skin, trying to focus on my surroundings. Then, realizing where I was, I laid myself back down and slept the remainder of the night without a reoccurrence of any nightmares.

I returned Larry's call the following day.

30

I listened quietly as Larry slung questions at me about the arrest. "I heard you were arrested after you left Johnny's the other night. What happened? Did you tell them anything? Was my name ever mentioned?" Without concern for my well being he rattled on. I got the distinct impression the only reason for his call was that his own anonymity as drug dealer had been protected.

I regurgitated the story to him. Whatever I said seemed to appease his fear. We put my incarceration to rest and talked briefly about nothing in particular. The conversation was light and comfortable. I took the opportunity to set up a time when we could meet and maybe begin where we left off or maybe we could start over. One thing I did not realize was that I would never be able to go back to the way things were again. "If you have some time next week I'd love to see you," I asked with anticipation of rejection already forming in my mind.

"O.K. I'll give you call in a few days and we'll arrange a time that works. Good luck in court. I'll talk to you later," he said.

His acceptance of my suggestion placed me on cloud nine. My fear of rejection completely disintegrated, and I began fantasizing about our next interlude.

31

The sun was shining brilliantly through my bedroom. The sheer white drapes that covered my window may as well of been nonexistent. I lay yawning on my back, patiently waiting for the sleepy haze of the night to lift from my head. I stretched, raising my arms above my head and forcing my legs to reach for the wall beyond the bed. The alarm clock continued to buzz on my nightstand. I reached above my head and switched it off. It was 6:30 a.m. Today I would stand before the judge accused of a crime I did commit. I arose from bed.

I had meticulously planned my attire for my court appearance in anticipation of a male judge. I quickly bathed and dressed. I could feel a nervous twinge in my abdominal area. I tried to convince myself I was just hungry, but in my heart I knew better. I had a couple of run ins with the law in my youth. I recognized the fear. A familiar feeling. I could be made an example of, or the judge could take mercy on a first time offender. Whatever the punishment, the simple fact remained that my fate lay in the hands of a stranger.

I had asked Janis to accompany me to court today. I was too nervous to drive. I knew the company of my friend would be a good distraction on the drive to Downey . It would keep me out of my head, my fear, and my thoughts. I heard a tap on the my bedroom door.

"Come on, Louise, it's time to go. You don't want to be late," Janis urged

"I'm ready," I yelled as I slipped on my shoes, and checked my purse for all the necessary documents I would need in court. Satisfied, I met Janis at the door.

The courthouse was a straight shot west on Imperial Avenue. We arrived fifteen minutes before my appearance was scheduled. We parked the car and proceeded to the room that held my case on the docket. Janis and I found two seats in the front row and waited for my name to be called.

The judge appeared in his early sixties. I observed quietly how he handled the cases before mine. He was firm yet fair. He commanded respect from the attorneys at the tables. Although the robe projected a powerful authoritarian figure, his eyes divulged the kindness and compassion of my grandfather.

I was called to appear before the judge. He asked if I had representation.

"No, your honor. I would like a public defender," I requested. My hands were trembling slightly, but it wasn't noticeable to on lookers. I stood erect, clothed in a pale pink cotton skirt that fell at mid thigh level, a black sleeveless blouse that V-ed at the neck line. The cut ended just above my cleavage and a long sleeve, waist length blazer black with pale pink pin stripes. I had removed all my jewelry. I was attempting to project a simple persona with a touch of sensuality that would appeal to the male libido.

"Miss Tote, at this time you may meet with a public defender to determine if you qualify for this service. I'll grant a continuance to a week from tomorrow at which time you may have counsel present. Next case," the judge ordered.

I let out a sigh of relief. As I turned to walk away from the podium, a public defender approached me and asked that I follow him. I followed him to a small cubicle just off the main court room. A four by six table and four folding chairs inhabited the room.

"Please, have a seat Miss Tote. My name is James Dewitt. If you qualify, I will be your attorney. There are a few questions I need to ask you. What I will be doing is determining your financial status. Now, are you employed? If so, where?" he asked.

I answered his questions. With each answer he jotted something down on a legal pad in front of him. He wore a full beard and mustache, which made it difficult to determine his age. My guess was he was some where between thirty-eight and forty-five. He wore wire framed spectacles that slipped down his nose with each downward tilt of the head. Each time he would diligently push them back into place. His hair was mousy brown and cut in no particular style. It hung slightly below his ears. He was dressed in a cheap, three-piece dark gray suit. After the completion of the questions and forms, he looked at me. He seemed to be pondering something. I waited silently for his conclusion.

"Well, according to what you have told me and how you answered the questions, you do not qualify for a public defender. Although your income is modest, you fall into a range in which the state does not consider you indigent. Therefore, you are able to pay your own legal fees." He spoke in a monotone voice as he rejected my request.

I sat with my hands clenched together, uncertainty written on my face. " I'm sorry, I don't understand. Basically what you're telling me is if I did not have a job, if I lived off the graciousness of the state, I would qualify for a public defender. That does not seem fair. I cannot afford an attorney, if I could I would not be here," my voice quivered as I pleaded, with as much dignity as I could muster. "Sir, I need your help! Please?"

"Let me look at your case." He looked through the report and the charges quickly. " Since this is your first offense, my legal advice is to plead no contest to the charge of under the influence and not guilty to driving under the influence. The latter charge will, in all probability, be dropped. A plea of no contest is not admitting or denying guilt, but be willing to do what the judge deems necessary for restitution of your actions. You will be fined, put on probation and required to do some type of rehabilitation program. You will not lose your driver's license. You'll be fine if you follow my advice when you appear before the judge next week. Any questions?" He passed me the documents of my case and left me sitting alone in the cubicle.

I took a deep breath, gathered the papers and found Janis who was sitting outside the court room waiting patiently.

"Well?" she asked as we walked toward the exit of the court house.

I reiterated everything the public defender had told me and added with some relief, " It seems the punishment for under the influence of drugs is not as harsh as a charge involving alcohol. "

The day was warming slightly from the earlier morning hour. We drove back to the apartment after making a quick stop at Del Taco for some $.59 cent burritos. We knew we would never starve with a food deal like that at our finger tips.

Janis dropped me at home, took her burrito and headed out to visit some friends. I spent the remainder of the afternoon mentally pondering the events in the courtroom and the suggestions of the attorney before I left for work that evening.

-32-

The following day I called Larry. I told him about my experience at the courthouse and what I perceived based on what the public defender told me would be the final outcome of the case. He listened silently. I could not even hear him breathing through the receiver. After a short conversation we made plans to spend some time together soon.

Over the next three weeks, I spent one night with Larry. I managed to ease my way back into his bed. We made love intensely and passionately for hours one evening. It was as if no time had lapsed between our encounters of love making. He brought me to levels of ecstasy I had only read about. His intuitive ability to read my body, bringing me to multiple orgasms, amazed me as I lay naked wrapped in his arms, sweaty and exhausted. His breath blew on my neck as he slept soundly after our interlude. I slowly drifted off.

My sleep was invaded by horrible images that eluded me in my awakened state, but my body was still quivering. I lifted my body from the bed, quickly dressed, kissed Larry lightly on the lips so as not to wake him and left.

I was unable to shake the unnerving feeling the dream left inside of me. "What was my psyche trying to reveal?" I asked myself.

-33-

The spring quarter had begun four weeks ago. I was finally starting to see some light at the end of the tunnel. One more year and I'd complete the necessary requirements for my Bachelors in Accounting. But I was finding it difficult to stay focused on my college work. It was seeming less and less important, while Larry was becoming more of a central focus and a distraction He invaded my thoughts, but I would manage to pull off acceptable grades during my last quarter at Cal State San Bernardino.

One week prior to the quarter ending, I gave the management at El Gato Gordo two week's notice. I could work more shifts at the Whole Enchilada if I needed the money.

The spring quarter ended the week before Memorial Day weekend, the beginning of summer. It would also be the summer of a radical, unpredictable, life altering change.

With the school year about finished, I had already planned my Memorial Day weekend vacation. Mitch and I once shared a seventeen foot prowler travel trailer at the Colorado river. We decided to split the cost and time equally. The summer consisted of four major holidays and we would each chose two holidays. Memorial weekend was my time to partake in the festive River activities, the boating, jet skiing, drinking and drugging.

Larry and I loaded the truck with food, beer, and few articles of clothes Thursday evening. We would leave once Rick came by and dropped off some "pink." The summer heat staggered into the night. The crescent moon dangled singularly in the sky from our view. Our relationship appeared to be advancing in a direction I found fulfilling. I was back in the inner circle, which is what I had wished for. What it meant to be allowed back in, I had no idea. With excitement in my heart and meth in my veins, we hit the highway towards Parker, Arizona. Darin would be tending to business at the house while we vacationed.

Mitch had called me earlier that day and asked if I minded if he tented on the space where we would have the trailer.

"Of course you're welcome, but let me slide it by Larry so there are no problems. Are you sure you're going to be O.K. with seeing Larry and me together?"

"I'll be fine. I just need a little vacation."

I called Mitch back and gave him an affirmative on his request.

Larry removed the top of the truck, and as we drove further away from the city and closer to our destination, the tapestry of night began to change. I tilted my head back against the seat and gazed at the heavens above. I could still taste the bitterness of the meth in my mouth, but nothing could take away from the magic of the night. The cassette player was jamming with Guns n' Roses and filled my ears. A cinema of stars began to dance above my head, accompanied by the moon on a black canvas. What little moisture was in the air had dissipated upon entering the desert, creating a dry, warm breeze. I sipped a cold beer as we traveled down Rice road. I was absorbed in the totality of the moment.

We pulled into to River Land at about three in the morning. Larry switched the radio off as we drove to our space where the trailer had been placed by the staff of the resort. We had a river front space in the middle of the camp. The camp was located in Earp, California along the Colorado River. The water front spaces consisted of cabanas and a picnic table under the covering. We knew approximately twenty people who would be spending the weekend at River Land. He began connecting the water and the sewage hose. I plugged the electricity in, proceeded to open the trailer and unload the supplies.

Mitch, Danny and a few other of our friends began arriving the following day. The next couple of days were spent in a mind altered haze. Our friends would come in and out of the trailer seeking refuge to do their dope, in order to remain undetected by those who did not find our way of life appropriate or acceptable. We spent hours cruising up river and drifting back in the boat. The boat was a twenty-three foot day cruiser belonging to Danny's dad. So far, it was like every other River vacation I had taken except the company I kept. Until the last day there.

"Hey, anyone want to go for a boat ride?" Danny asked "My dad's letting me take the boat for the afternoon. Come on." He said, as he waved us towards the boat.

Larry, Mitch, and I, along with five others piled in the boat. We sped up river, as soon as we were out of eye shot of the parents. Larry headed down to the cabin. "Anyone want one? Come on down." He yelled over the sound the engine.

One by one we gratefully accepted. To us, it was a religious undertaking, like taking holy communion and Larry was the priest, for that moment. The engine started to sputter at the same time Larry was making his way up top. "What's going on?" Larry asked.

"I don't know, man, but I am losing power. Pull the engine cover up and check it out, Larry." Danny replied. Everyone stared around with blank looks in there eyes, while Larry fiddled with the engine.

"Maybe we are out of gas, guys. Danny didn't I hear your Dad tell you to fill the tank while we were out? I asked.

Larry glared at me from over his shoulder and said, " I think you should keep your mouth shut and let us handle it."

"But, Larry, I am just trying to help. Especially since no one has checked the obvious. Hello!" I sarcastically retorted.

"I suggest you shut up, now," he said vehemently.

His face looked twisted and contorted as he ordered me to stay in my place. I managed to stay quiet, until Danny yelled, "You guys won't believe this, but we're out of gas. Can someone throw the bumpers out? I'll try to guide the boat to the dock over there," he said, pointing across the river.

I said, " I told you so." The words slipped out of my mouth in a hostile and condescending tone, before I could think about what I was saying. As the last word left my lips, I immediately saw the rage in Larry's eyes, and I moved to the other side of the boat. I was confident his anger would pass once we had gas in the boat and could continue where we left off. In the meantime, I kept my distance.

We pulled up to the site at River Land a couple of hours later, extremely drunk and sunburned. I stayed behind to wipe the boat down and haul the trash to shore. Although I thought Larry had cooled down, I wanted to make sure.

That evening, I passed on dinner, and instead began pumping my system with niacin in hopes of flushing the drugs out of my body. We were leaving tomorrow, and the following day, Tuesday I had to report to a facility to begin my drug diversion program. Part of the program was initial drug testing. That was part of my sentence handed down by the judge for my arrest in April. Larry sat silently at the table, fiddling with an RC car, a recent hobby for him. As I came out of the bathroom, the niacin made me feel weak and disoriented. Nausea waved through my abdominal area, but there was no food to remove, causing dry heaves. I sat down across from Larry. He did not acknowledge me.

"I don't feel good. Larry, would you please make me a quesadilla?" I asked.

"Make your own dam quesadilla. There isn't anything wrong with you," He coldly stated.

"I told you I had to take the niacin today and it is making sick, please Larry, I feel like I am going to pass out. It will only take a minute," I pleaded, but he did not respond. "Larry are you still mad about today? If you are, I am sorry."

"Bitch, just shut up! I'm not making you any food, so quit acting like a cry baby and leave me alone. I am busy, " he shouted.

I moved away from the table and crawled into bed. Drawing myself into a fetal position, I managed to get a few hours of rest. When I woke, Larry was still in the same place, doing the same thing as he was when I went to sleep.

"Good morning," I softly said.

"Yeah, whatever," he greeted in return.

I got out of bed, I walked over to Larry, and I kissed him on the cheek. He winced as my lips touched his face. Without saying another word, I walked to the bathroom and continued my morning routine. The next few hours were void of conversation. I was at a loss for words. We would be leaving in a few hours, so I began to pack. Although I cautiously maneuvered around Larry, somehow I still managed to push his buttons marked anger, rage, hate and fear.

"What the hell are you doing?" he asked.

"I'm packing your clothes," I said.

"Don't touch my stuff. I can pack it," he said. Simultaneously he stood up and walked over to me and pushed me on the floor.

"All right, I was just trying to be helpful. You didn't have to push me. I wasn't hurting anything," I said as the tears were beginning to drip from my eyes.

"If I want to push, you will. Do you hear me?" he screamed in my face, while shoving his finger in my chest. Then he turned and stormed out the door.

He was quickly becoming an internal infernal tower of rage.

I remained inside the trailer. I heard a knock on the trailer door. "Come in," I said.

"Is everything all right? I saw Larry come out, and he looks fit to be tied," my friend, Vicki, asked.

"I don't know what is going on with him," I said. Then I replayed her the events of the evening and morning. I found it difficult to speak at times through the sobbing, but she patiently listened.

"I don't think you should ride home with him," she said.

"I don't want to, but how else will I get home?" I asked.

"You could ride with me, Mitch, or Danny. Any of us will give you a ride," she said.

"O.K., that would be great. Thank you so much, I really appreciate it," I said. A sense of relief swept through me when I realized there was another alternative. I sat on the floor and began packing my bag as Vicki waited inside with me. No longer were the tears streaming down my face.

The trailer door slammed open and Larry stood in the door way. "What do you think you are doing?" he asked.

From where I was sitting, Larry appeared threatening as he looked down on me, like a deranged giant out of a bad horror movie. "I am going home with Vicki," I responded.

"Do you think that I am going to let you humiliate me, then leave with someone else? Do you?" he asked with uncanny calmness. He had bent towards me so he was a couple of inches from my face. I could feel the moisture from his breath against my skin as he waited for an answer. I was stunned at the calmness in his demeanor when he spoke, it was spooky. I suddenly was verbally debilitated.

"Well, I am waiting for an answer." he said. "Are you afraid of me?" he asked. He now had a hint of sarcasm in his tone.

"Uh, no I am not afraid of you, you have just been acting so weird, it is freaking me out, " I said, "I told you I was sorry about yesterday."

I felt his hand suddenly reach down and grab a clump of hair on the upper left side of my head. He yanked my body towards his, using my hair as his handle. "So you thought you'd ride home with someone else. I don't think so, " he stated as he dragged me across the floor like rag doll.

I reached my hands above my head to grab on to his arm, in order to gain some leverage and reduce the pain I was feeling in my head as strands of hair were being torn from the scalp. "Larry, stop! Your hurting me! " I yelled through my sobs.

He proceeded to drag me across the trailer floor. I flailed my legs around helplessly as I tried to regain my balance from the sudden attack. I caught a glimpse of my friend's eyes. Fear and helplessness beamed across her face, as she yelled "Stop it! Stop it!" He released me from his grip, shaking all the torn hair from his hand.

"We are leaving in ten minutes. You had better be ready," he said and casually walked out the door.

I sat sobbing on the floor where he had dropped me. I looked blankly at Vicki. Finally able to stop the tears, I reassured her I would be all right.

"Please don't worry about me. It will be better if I go with him. I don't want to drag anyone else into this shit, especially since I don't have a clue what it is about. He is like Dr. Jeckle and Mr. Hyde. I have never seen him like this,"I said.

I stepped outside to throw my bag in the truck when I noticed a crowd of friends had gathered outside the trailer. I stopped dead in my tracks and I looked directly at Mitch, who was sitting on the picnic table bench near the trailer. He spoke to me in a gentle, confused manner "Louise, what is going on? We heard crying, yelling, and saw the trailer moving about erratically. You don't look so good."

Embarrassed and ashamed that my friends were witness to this attack, I pushed back the tears. With a deep seeded need to convince myself and Mitch, I tried to explain away the incident as a normal dispute between lovers. "Larry and I were just having an argument. It is no big deal. Everything is fine. Really, I'll be fine."

Mitch walked over to me, wrapped his arms around me in friendship and love, and whispered, "You know you don't have to go with him. You may not be safe."

Pulling away from his embrace, I looked towards Larry, who was waiting in the truck a few feet away observing us. "You could do me a really big favor. Can you lock up the trailer and make sure everything is secure so the park people can haul it back to its storage space? I would appreciate it. I have to go," I told Mitch.

Everyone else remained silent during this exchange of words. They sat motionless as I walked past, head hung down and climbed into the passenger seat of the truck.

Larry remained quiet for the first half hour of the trip home. Although the night air was warm, I could not rid myself of the internal chill. I desperately tried to communicate with him. "Larry, please tell me what is going on. Why are you so mad at me, please?" I begged.

When he finally did speak only hateful words escaped his lips. "Shut-up, you know what you did to deserve what happened earlier," he said.

"What are you talking about? You're crazy!" I yelled. Abruptly he yanked the wheel to his right and headed into the middle of the desert.

My head ached from crying and having my hair pulled so violently from its follicles. I screamed to be heard above the wind and the sound of the desert fauna under the tires. "What the hell are you doing, now!" With that he slammed on the brakes, lurching my body forward.

"Get out! Get the hell out!" he screamed.

I was unable to react with anything other than sobs, paralyzed by shock from what I was hearing. Finally I found my voice when I saw him get out of the truck and move towards my door in an effort to make his point very clear. "What? You can't be serious. You can't leave me out here in the middle of night!"

He opened the door, grabbed my arm and yanked me out of truck, causing me to fall on the hard desert floor. I landed on a small cactus and abrasive desert soil. I yelped in pain as the needles punctured my flesh. "Yes I can and that is exactly what I'm doing." He walked back to the driver's side and threw out my duffel bag. I was pleading and begging to return with him when he pulled away into the night.

I remained seated where I had fallen, sobbing, I began to pray to an uncertain and ill defined power. I could hear the crickets chirping and the coyotes howling off in the distance. I became increasingly more fearful for my safety as the minutes ticked away and I sat there feeling completely vulnerable and exposed to the environment.

Being left in the desert was more terrifying to me than riding home with Larry at this moment. Only a half hour had passed when I heard the roar of the a four wheel drive engine.

"God, let it be Larry," I pleaded earnestly.

Spraying me with desert soil, he halted inches in front of me. "Get in the truck, and I don't want to hear another word from your mouth," he ordered.

I reverted instantly to that child that had just received punishment for some wrongdoing and meekly climbed into the truck. Larry peeled out on to Rice Road. The two lane highway was completely deserted. I remained silent as I had been told to for the remainder of the journey. My hair stung my skin as it whipped across my face, thoughts of escape whirling around in my head. When we get back to Diamond Bar, I can just jump in my car and go home. I can forget this ever happened, I continued to tell myself.

We pulled into his driveway. Before I realized what was happening Larry had me by the arm was removing me from the truck and forcibly leading me upstairs. He shoved me into the bedroom and locked the doors.

I stood closed in his room, a prisoner of his rage. "Let me out of here. I just want to go home!" I yelled through the door, while I fumbled with the door knob

With no response, I scoured the vanity table for some dope. When all else failed in my life, I knew at least I could depend on "the pink" to further suppress my emotions. I found enough for a line and quickly snorted it. The saltiness of my tears blended with the bitterness of the drugs in my mouth. I snapped my attention away from my thoughts when I heard a key slipped into the lock. I ran to the door. His body blocked the door frame, preventing my escape. He shoved me back and locked the door. Huddled on the floor, I watched as he began stripping his clothes off. I recoiled at the thought of what was about to happen. I was thirteen all over again.

He moved towards me and yanked at my tank top. I tried with all the physical strength I could gather to shove him away from me. He may as well have been a two thousand pound object for all the good my retaliation did. My top ripped off. He groped and pinched at my flesh. I went limp. I felt like a rag doll. I stopped fighting back, because it only increased his forcefulness. I shut down every sense and reverted into my own inner world as this demoralizing act took place against my body. When he was through, he rolled over and went to sleep. Paralyzed, I stared blankly at the ceiling in the pitch black of night and tried to justify his behavior in my head. Eventually I slept.

I felt an arm fall across my chest. A tender kiss on my cheek. I began moving from my dream state to consciousness. The previous night's events came flooding back as I felt Larry's lips pressing against my skin. I shrank away from his touch. I opened my eyes to look at him. I felt apprehensive and confused.

"Good morning, sweetie," he uttered in my ear

"Uh, morning," I had difficulty absorbing the abrupt change of character and the complete lack of acknowledgment of his cruel, violent behavior. When I stared into his eyes a softness shown through and an innocent boyish aura surrounded him. Was it merely what I wanted to see, or had there been a complete transformation during the night? Or had my perception of the situation been an illusion of the reality of the events? Was I insane? These questions arose in my mind. I found myself unable to be objective and see the rape and abuse for what it was, which was a violent assault against my persons. Instead, I buried the hurt, the anger, the pain and the shame so deep in my soul I never spoke of it again. I placed myself in an arena of complete denial, irrationality and insanity.

Once I made the decision to push the experience away, it was easy for me to reciprocate the tenderness Larry bestowed upon me. I just wanted to believe. I returned home later that afternoon.

I canceled my appointment to meet with drug diversion counselor for a later date, since I knew if a urine test was administered the results would be positive.

-35-

I sat on my bed attempting to comb out the strands of hair. Between torn fragments coupled with the wind whipping through it on the return trip from the river, my hair had turned into one large dread lock. Unable to make any progress on that project I pulled out the phone book and began browsing through the yellow pages in the restaurant section.

I wanted to get an idea of what local places existed. I had decided to begin seeking other employment. My position at El Gato Gordo had been terminated May 24th due to my inexcusable tardiness on Mother's Day, which was the restaurant's busiest day of the year. Prior to the release of my duties, I had given my two week notice. The drive to Riverside was interfering with my free time. With the school year ending, there was absolutely no reason for me to continue making the drive. I just was asked to leave a week earlier than I expected.

I was making a list of various restaurants to call when Janis came home.

"Hey, Louise, are you home?" she yelled.

"Yeah, I'm in my room. Come on in," I answered, still sitting on my bed.

Entering my room she looked at me quizzically and asked, "What happened to your hair, girlfriend? It's a mess."

Stating half truths, I replied, "The wind had matted it during the long drive home, and I didn't try combing it out before I went to sleep last night."

"Mmmm, let me take a look." Sitting down next to me trying to pull the strands gently apart, she said, "What happened here? Your missing a large patch of hair." She touched the area where the strands no longer existed.

I made up some ridiculous story that she didn't question, but I knew she didn't believe it either. She let me keep my secret to myself, and there it stayed.

As she continued to try and bring my hair to its original form, we talked about our weekends. "I'm not having much luck here. I may have to cut about four or five inches off in order to remove all the damaged areas. Why don't you come in the shop this week. I'll see what I can do. The question is, once I get it detangled will it look healthy?"

"I really do not want to cut it. Just let me know when to come in and I'll be there," I said with much hesitation.

"It would look great if you let me cut it just below your shoulders. How come you do not want to cut it?" she asked.

"I have this short hair phobia. When I was six or seven, my aunt hacked my beautiful shag cut into a pixie cut. The following Sunday, after church, my mom to took me to the grocery store and as we were walking out I heard a boy ask his mom why a boy was wearing a dress, referring to me. I was crushed and I cried all day. Right then, I promised myself I would never let anyone cut my hair short again, and so far, that promise hasn't been broken," I said.

"Well, I'll work on it later and see if at least I can get most of the tangles out. I have to run some errands. I'll see you later."

Janis managed to detangle it after hours of combing and pulling. Although it looked extremely unhealthy and straggly, I was still hesitant to let her cut it.

-36-

During the next couple of weeks, the incident that took place at the River seemed like a nightmare, and I woke to find it was nothing more than my imagination. The relationship was taking a fairy tale turn. We discussed the idea of moving in together. Of course, I would move in to his house. We shared extraordinary hours making love. I chose to base the progress or demise of our union on the sexual relationship we shared. It was continually escalating in upward direction during this brief period. That was the only way I was able to connect on an emotional level with Larry, so I was in heaven. In retrospect, what a distorted perception of love I had.

Rick remained an integral part of our lives. He was placed high on a pedestal in our minds; he was omnipotent. Not only did he supply us with "the pink", our social activities centered around him. Our attachment, our friendship, and our addiction grew stronger to the point of psychosis the more time we spent with Rick.

Darin was the final link of this intimate, obscure inner circle of four. There were others who were allowed in to the outer circle that surrounded the inner ring, but the make up of that was constantly changing. The four of us remain strangely connected while all else shifted and turned around us.

Today, I was supposed to pay Larry for the sixteenth I had fronted for a friend, last week. But before I went to his house I had an interview at Bobby McGee's, a bar and restaurant in Brea. Dressed in a black with pink pin stripe pants suit, which I had borrowed from Carol, I turned left onto the Orangethorpe on ramp of the 57 Freeway heading north. A large construction wall was erected as a barrier to the right of the ramp. It seemed that for as long as I could remember, the city had been working on this ramp. The wall made the ramp seem uncomfortably narrow and short and did not allow a car to gain the necessary speed to merge into traffic safely. A white Aerostar van preceded me onto the ramp. As we reached the flow of traffic, I turned my head to the left and began to move the wheel in the same direction, easing the car onto the freeway. I turned my head back to the car in front of me. Red brake lights gleamed at me. Without any reaction time possible, my body jolted forward. My head smashed against the rear view mirror, cracking it, when the right front end of my car collided with the van in front of me. My body slammed back into the bucket seat when the motion of the collision came to a halt. Shaken, it took me a moment to process what had just happened. I had been in an accident.

I saw a Middle-Eastern looking man step out of the van and begin walking towards me, angrily shaking his finger at me shouting things I could not understand. I stepped out of my car to assess the damage and confront the idiot who had come to dead halt at the end of the on ramp when freeway traffic had been a steady flow. Damage to the van was minimal; the Camaro seemed to incur the worst of it. After a short verbal confrontation, he left the scene, not wanting to file a police report. I returned to my car, started the engine, and hobbled to the next off ramp. I found a gas station near the exit with a pay phone. Still shaken from the experience, I cradled the phone on my shoulder because my hand was too shaky to hold the receiver steadily. I called David, a friend who worked for a body shop, and who had done some work on my car a few months prior. I told David about the accident and he said he would be down immediately in a tow truck. Once we returned to the body shop he would arrange for a rental car. I sat on the black top and waited patiently for David to arrive. "Well, I guess I'll miss the interview," I thought to myself. "Oh, well."

Within an hour, I was back at the body shop and on my way to pick up a rental car.

I pulled out of the Enterprise rent a car lot and headed to Larry's. I wanted some comfort from the day's events. I wanted to feel his arms wrapped around me and his hands gently stroke my hair. Just the thought of me in his embrace brought me an internal warmth. I pulled the car along the curb in front of Larry's house. I hastily made my way to the front door. After a few minutes of insistent ringing of the door bell, Larry yelled, "Who is it?"

"It's me."

His hair was ruffled from sleep and he wore only a pair of faded blue jeans.

"Come in, " he said. Then he peered outside. "Where is your car?"

I told him I was in an accident while I trailed behind him up the stairs to the master bedroom.

"Oh, well do you have my money?" he asked, flopping down on the bed.

I stunned by his lack of compassion. Irritation arose inside me. I'll show him. If his damn money is more important than me, I won't give it to him.

"No, I don't have your money!" I screamed, "And you may never get it." I turned and ran down the stairs. I could hear footsteps pounding behind me. I reached the front door, flung it open and continued to run to my car, but before I could get in the driver's seat Larry was upon me.

He forcibly grabbed my forearm and spun me around.

"You're hurting me, let go," I wailed. A sharp sting spread across my cheek.

"Listen bitch, you had better give me my money now or there is more where that came from," he stated with an eerie calm tone that had a recent sound of familiarity.

I had no doubt he would hold true to his statement. I reached for my wallet and removed the money. He released his grip the moment I handed it to him.

With a kiss on the cheek he said, "Thanks, but I have some business to take care of so I think you should go. I'll call you later." As if nothing had happened, he returned to the house.

I sat in my car before driving away, trying to digest what had just happened. "Maybe I did deserve that." I thought, which would be my mantra for the months to follow." After all, it was his money. It wasn't his fault I was in an accident. He has his own worries. I cannot expect him to put everything aside to comfort me, can I?" said the insecure, unworthy girl inside my head. I shoved the anger down into the bottom of my soul and replaced it with self doubt because that was all I knew how to do. I had years of practice blaming myself for others' unacceptable behavior and inability to show love in a healthy manner, formulating the feelings, or lack thereof, into logic a child could grasp. " I must be a bad girl." It made perfect sense in my mind.

By the time I reached my apartment, that day had been translated by my psyche into a day that was deserving to a person such as myself, whatever that self may be. I didn't have a clue. I felt exhausted from the day as night blanketed the city in darkness. I would take my cue from the descent of the sun and do the same. " I'll start over tomorrow. It will be a better day," I tried to convince myself as I slipped my clothes off to prepare for bed.

Sleep came quickly, but with it came another dream or what some would call a nightmare.

I woke to the phone ringing. I stretched my arm above my head to the night stand and located the phone.

"Hello," I answered sleepily

"Good morning, sunshine."

"What time is it?" I asked as I began to do my wake up cat stretch, starting at my toes and working my way up.

"It's about 8:30 a.m. I didn't mean to wake you. I thought you might be getting ready for work already. Anyway, I was just thinking about you. I miss you. Why don't you come over tomorrow after work. I'd love to see you," Larry said with the genuine enthusiasm of a man missing his beloved.

" O.K. tomorrow sounds great. I only work the afternoon shift, so I'll be over around 6:00. By the way, I miss you too. See you later."

"Until then," he said.

I let the phone drop from my hand onto the bed as I stretched my upper body before rising. "Yesterday was just one of those off days. We all have them. I knew today would be a better day." I conversed in my mind as the excitement grew inside my stomach at the thought of seeing Larry tomorrow.

-37-

It was a sunny day in June . The ocean breezes blew the smog out of the inland valley. The sky was crystal blue. Work at The Whole Enchilada was unusually slow during this late afternoon. The regular afternoon customers were most likely enjoying the beautiful outdoors. My boss invited me to go to happy hour with him at local bar up the street. Vince, the owner and my boss, was a handsome man in his early forties, but with the spirit and vitality of a twenty year old. Hair the color of salt and pepper, but with double the amount of pepper and cut in an executive style. A dark thick mustache resided on his upper lip. He was a kind, fair man, but when his temper flared, we all ran for cover. Only on two occasions in the six years I had worked there did that occur. He was always dressed in casual professional business attire, a Ralph Lauren polo and dress slacks. I eagerly accepted his invitation for happy hour at the Acapulco bar. Before I headed out the door, I called Larry to let him know of my plans and that I would be by in a couple of hours. I went with his blessing. After a few top shelve marguaritas and giddy conversation, I left the bar. I stood still on the steps outside the bar. I slipped my Ray Bans on, while I allowed my eyes to adjust to the light of dusk. Feeling a little light headed and euphoric from the tequila, I took two deep breaths and walked to my car. I started the engine, turned the radio on and began to sing along with my favorite rock bands. I headed towards Larry's speeding south on Diamond Bar Boulevard at seventy miles an hour.

The dusk had turned to darkness. The darkness, the night cloaked me. It absorbed and penetrated my being. Within its confines I could create my greatest illusions. Rolling both windows down in my rented Camry, I created a wind tunnel. The wind whipped my hair across my face at moments, making it difficult to see the road ahead. It didn't matter, I could drive Diamond Bar Blvd. blindfolded. The car seemed to drive itself to Larry's. I arrived at his house within ten minutes. Rejuvenated and intoxicated I trotted up to Larry's front door and let myself in. Immediately I spotted Larry amongst some friends in the living room. I ran up to Larry threw my arms around his neck, and pressed my lips against his.

Jostled by my sudden appearance, he untangled my arms from around his neck with an excessive amount of force. He moved to me arms distance from him.

"You've been drinking," he scowled as he took a sip of the Budweiser in his hand.

"Yes," I giggled, "what else would I be doing at happy hour?"

His expression portrayed disgust and anger. His eyes revealed loathing from the very bottom of his soul. I quickly turned away from him to greet our friends. I picked up an unopened can of beer from the table, popped the tab and took a large gulp. I sat on the coffee table my back facing Larry in hopes of shielding myself from his bitterness. I asked, "What are we going to do this evening?"

Robert, a mutual friend, said, "Let's go over to my house. Play cards and darts or whatever."

I turned to Larry who was nodding in acceptance to Robert's offer. I excused myself from the group and headed up the stairs to the master bedroom. Seating myself at the vanity table, I pulled the drawer open and removed a mirror, a razor blade and the stash from inside. I opened the seal and removed a small amount of the contents and placed it on the mirror. Already anticipating the feeling I quickly drew a line. As I inhaled, my eyes immediately began to water. I grabbed the bridge of my nose, an involuntary reaction to the burning sensation I felt. I moaned quietly with satisfaction and replaced the paraphernalia to its designated home. I grabbed the edge of the vanity to regain my balance from the abrupt motion of standing. I checked my appearance in the mirror to insure no remnants of the drug lingered on the edge of my nostrils. Satisfied, I returned down stairs.

Larry returned to socializing with his friends. Although appearing agitated by my unannounced interruption, he was able to gather his outward composure when I headed upstairs. He raised his voice in order to tune out the inner dispute. His friends became aware of the abrupt change in his demeanor, but were unable to predict what would take place the following hour. Slowly everyone filed out of the house, as each reaffirmed they would all meet at Robert's condo.

Larry watched me float down the stairs, as he mechanically nodded affirmations to his friends. Clad in a light blue pin striped sleeveless summer dress with buttons closing the dress around my bodice extending to my mid thigh. The top button was left undone revealing the upper curve of my breasts. A simple pair of patent leather white pumps accentuated my slender legs. For a moment, he looked adoringly at me, but that passed quickly.

" How could she go out and drink with another man, especially dressed like that? Action such as this must be punished!" his committee screamed. The voices echoed the words so loudly he looked to see if anyone else seemed to hear it. Everyone was oblivious to his tormentor, as he would share with me at a later date.

Having finished my descent, I stood next to Larry and waved to the last of the group as they headed out the door. Flickers of rage shone through his placid blue eyes. All the boyish qualities in his facial features vanished the instant he turned to me and spoke. " Let's go." I followed closely behind Larry as we headed outside to the car.

An uneasiness filled the car. Larry drove silently. Once he had pulled the car out of the cul-de-sac and began heading north on Diamond Bar Blvd, he broke the silence.

"What were you doing out with your boss?" he yelled.

" Having a couple of drinks. What's eating you?" I responded, attempting to maintain a calm demeanor.

The distance to Robert's condo was five miles from Larry's house, but the ten minute drive was beginning to seem like an eternity. The tone of his voice continued to escalate during his interrogation. I attempted to defend my actions. I lost my cool. He pulled into the Allegro condo complex parking lot. He was pulling into a visitor's space when "Fuck you!" screeched from my lips.

Without warning, I felt a sudden sting across my left cheek. Larry had backhanded me. I could feel the reddening process immediately.

Glaring at him I hissed, "Enjoy your evening. Get out of my car."

"You're coming with me," he said.

" I will not!"

Grabbing my long hair, pulling my head to his lips he hissed, " We will drive to the liquor store and then we are coming back together. Do you understand me?"

Although his violent, erratic behavior had revealed itself before, I was nonetheless stunned by Larry's sudden outburst. I had painted the red flags green that led up to this point. He put the car in reverse and backed out of the visitor's stall. The realization of what had just occurred was beginning to turn my fear into hatred. My mind whirled, no longer feeling the effects of the alcohol and drugs. Only rage penetrated my brain. I began to scream at him, hurling insults in order to hurt him. Larry only became more enraged by my outburst.

We made a right on to Diamond Bar Blvd. turning left on Grand Ave and left on Brea Canyon Road. He drove with his left hand on the steering wheel and his right hand firmly gripped around the back of my neck. His fingers sunk into my flesh. It felt as if my neck was in a vise, the grip continually being tightened with each attempt at resistance.

With a sudden abruptness I became silent. The pain forced me to retreat into the safe place of my mind, trying to assess the situation, but unable focus. Tears streamed down my cheeks, their warm saltiness washing past my lips. The taste was to familiar to my tongue. He abruptly jerked the wheel to the left and drove into the vacant parking lot next to the Mobile station mini mart. He slammed on the brakes, startling me.

My head came crashing down on the dashboard. Repeatedly, my face collided with the hard surface. Blood poured from my nostrils. I remained with my head resting on the dash board in hopes that the sudden attack would cease. His hand firmly gripped my hair in the same area that had already been damaged, eventually creating a larger bald area. What was happening?

His hand smashed against my skull. He hated me for making him see incompetence, his ignorance. He loved me for jarring his mind to other possibilities, for overlooking his lack of education, continuing to love him and stand by him. I would die for him. The line that divided these emotions became thinner with each passing day. They meshed together, defining one as the other in his mind.

"Had enough?" his voice echoed in my ears.

Instantly his fist collided with my face again and again. My eye began swelling shut. My lips swelled and turned blood red. My right hand groped for the door handle in hopes of escaping from this nightmare. Noticing my attempt to escape, he increased the intensity of the beating. The sound of my skull being smashed echoed in my ears. I was teetering on the edge of unconsciousness.

Then, as quickly as it had begun, it ceased. My body convulsed violently from the sobbing. I turned my head slowly to the left to see him step out of the driver's side door. The words he whispered in my ear rang clear. "Bitch don't fuck with me, next time you will have to be punished, and I will not stop with you. Your family will be next!" That one sentence induced a fear so intense that it permeated every cell, membrane and nerve of my being. The physical pain felt nonexistent. Through my blurred vision I could see Larry in the public phone booth to the right of the car with the receiver in his ear. I managed to get out of the car and approach him. I demanded my keys. He struck me once in the head with telephone receiver. I was dazed by the impact of the blow. He then threw the keys at me. I bent down to retrieve them, with the sudden realization of the beating I had just endured. " Fuck You!" spewed from my swollen lips as I staggered back to the car. Larry hung the receiver up and within five minutes Robert's car pulled up next to the phone booth.

Time seemed to stand still, but my thoughts raced as I tried to place the keys in the ignition, replaying the events of the last twenty minutes. Why had no one helped me? There had to have been many passersby, but they chose to be ignorant of this domestic dispute. No one had the courage to get involved. What was wrong with these people? What was wrong with me? What had I done to deserve such a brutal beating? Questions I could not answer.

The sharp thud of metal being kicked startled me. Slowly I lifted my head and looked through the windshield. Larry was violently waving his finger at me. I could see his lips moving, but the words were inaudible to me. His face had become contorted, taking on a demonic twist. Turning away from me, he strutted over to Robert's car and vanished.

-38-

Instinctively I knew I had to leave the parking lot. I turned the key in the ignition, and the engine began to purr. Shifting the car into drive, I made a right out of the lot onto Brea Canyon Road. I was grateful for the darkness and its protective cover of my wounds. I turned right on Grand, then right on Diamond Bar Blvd, then made a left into the Allegro Condo complex. I parked the car in a visitor's spot. Wrought with pain, I slowly walked to my friend Suzy's condo. I knew Suzy would have something to ease the pain and would require little explanation of the events that had put me in this condition. I could hear Led Zeppelin's "Stairway to Heaven" playing and the chatter of happy voices from somewhere inside the condo.

Suzy was a stunningly beautiful woman. Her hair a soft, natural blonde, flowed down the middle of her back, stopping above her tail bone. She had large oval shaped blue eyes, full of life. Her body was perfectly proportioned, slender and toned. Her skin glowed a golden color year around. Her vivacious and charming personality exceeded her beauty. She could make people laugh with her quick wit and jokes.

I had hired Suzy five years ago at the Whole Enchilada. The customers and her co-workers adored her. We became fast friends in a short period of time. Our bond grew stronger as time passed.

I rapped twice on the front door. Suzy yelled "Who is it?"

"Louise," I replied in a tone not much louder than a whisper. The sound of footsteps coming towards the door alarmed me. I didn't want my friend to see me like this. I didn't want anyone to see me in this humiliated battered state. As I was about to turn and run, Suzy swung the door open. Horror and concern flashed across her face. For a second Suzy was too stunned to speak. She motioned for me to come in. I stepped through the doorway. Suzy locked the door behind me. Turning to me she asked, "Did Larry do this to you?"

"Yes," I whispered.

Suzy, without hesitation, went to the linen closet, removed a hand towel and brought it to the kitchen, where I was now silently sitting. She soaked the towel with water and then began to cautiously clean my wounds in order that she might assess the extent of the damage to my face. Meekly, I asked for a beer. She reached inside of refrigerator, took out a Molson, opened it and handed it to me. Suzy continued to wipe the blood from my nose and lips until all that was left was a mass of bruising and swelling and a hollow, beaten girl. Suzy removed an ice pack from the freezer to help reduce the swelling.

I drained the Molson, asked for another and within minutes of receiving it, I had drained my second beer. The pain was beginning to numb like my soul. Suzy placed the ice pack on my eyes and continued this process for the next couple of hours over my entire face.

The garage was off the kitchen I could hear Suzy's husband, friends and the thud of the darts as they hit the board. Laughter seeped through the door into the kitchen. The door from the garage to the kitchen opened and James peered in to see where Suzy had disappeared. Noticing me at the kitchen table with my head cradled in my arms, he stepped into the kitchen. He tapped me on the shoulder. I lifted my head to look at him. Surprise filled his expression when he saw my blackened eyes, crooked nose, swollen lips and bruised cheeks. He knew instantly who had done this.

"Are you all right?" he asked.

"Yes," I replied.

"Where is he? I'll take care of him for you," he stated.

"No, I just want to forget about it," I responded.

"Is there anything I can do?" he asked.

"Yes here's some money. Can you go pick me up a gram?" I asked, reaching into my purse and withdrawing some bills.

He glanced over at Suzy who was sitting in the chair opposite me. She nodded her head in approval.

"O.K. I'll be back soon."

He made a quick telephone call and left. Within fifteen minutes James had returned. I felt my strength slowly returning. He handed me the baggy and some utensils. I thanked him and drew everyone a line. The drug produced the desired affect. Soon I was playing darts and laughing, managing to find some humor underneath the nightmare. All conversation about Larry was avoided. I avoided any mirrors and objects that created a reflection, a reminder of what had happened.

The night soon turned to dawn. Without any sleep, I was quickly becoming paranoid. All I wanted to do was go back to my apartment in Anaheim, but I was to afraid to drive. The shelter of the night sky was no longer there to protect me, from casual looks or from the policemen who might pass.

I convinced Suzy to drive me home and her husband would follow us in his car.

****

It was mid afternoon when I stepped into my apartment. Thank God no one was home. I closed and dead bolted the front door behind me. I went straight to my room. For the first time since the beating occurred, I faced the mirror over my vanity. My reflection was unrecognizable. A scared battered child stared back at me. Bruises were left along my cheek bones. The swelling had diminished slightly. Thick black and blue circles surrounded my empty brown eyes. My lips were slightly puffy with cuts on the inside of my lower lip from my teeth. My nose sat more to the right of my face than it had before. I turned my head away from the image in the glass. I couldn't bare to look anymore.

I moved to the corner of the room, stripped my clothes off, and tossed them in the trash as I did not want any reminders of last night. I eased myself down into the large brown bean bag. I wrapped my naked body in a blanket and curled up in a fetal position. Soon, I drifted off into a restless sleep.

-39-

Two days had passed since the beating. I managed to avoid my roommates. I didn't answer my door when they knocked. I only went out of my room when they were at work or out. I called in sick to work Sunday, and Monday I had the day off. I was unable to bear being seen by anyone, including my own eyes. The only dialogue that took place was in my head. "What is wrong with me? How come Larry hasn't called? What am I going to tell people when I go back to work Tuesday?"

The door slammed shut, jolting me from my thoughts.

"Is anyone home?" Janis yelled.

I could no longer continue to hide from Janis. Sleepily I responded. "In here, come on in."

Janis walked into my room. The room held the stillness and the darkness of night within its confines. Janis flipped the light switch on. She looked at me curled up on top of the bean bag in the corner of the room and thought the shadows were playing tricks on her eyes. Janis appeared confused. Then suddenly I remembered what an awful sight I must be. I quickly buried my head in the blanket that was wrapped around my body. Janis walked over to wear I was sitting and tugged the blanket away from my face.

"Oh my god!" escaped from Janis' lips.

I felt ashamed and embarrassed of my condition. Tears filled my eyes as I looked at Janis, unable to speak. Janis gently touched the bruises on my face with the tenderness of a mother towards her wounded child.

Looking into my teary eyes, Janis said, "You have to go the police, this guy is a lunatic."

My voice quivered as I pleaded with Janis. "You don't understand."

"What is there to understand? This man who you claim that cares about you has physically beaten you and you want to pretend that it didn't happen." Anger filled Janis' voice as she attempted to persuade me to take action.

Janis must have noticed a change in my eyes. They had become dull and filled with terror, because she stopped talking and waited patiently for an answer from me. I searched my mind for the right words to make Janis understand. Attempting to explain away Larry's cruel behavior, I took all the responsibility for the incident.

"It was my fault. I went out with my boss, had a little to much to drink and provoked him." I said, more for my sake than hers. I wanted to believe in him.

Janis swallowed her anger and hatred for Larry in order to convince me I didn't deserve be to treated in this manner. No act I could do would ever warrant such violence. Finally, I agreed to go down to the Walnut sheriff station, but only after Janis committed to driving me.

I quickly dressed in a pair of sweats, tank top and wind breaker. Fearful I would change my mind at any minute, we rushed out the door. The hallway outside our apartment was silent. The fluorescent lighting stung my eyes. I hung my head to hide the bruises from any neighbors who might pass by. Once in the elevator, Janis wrapped her arms around me and silently wept.

"You did not deserve this and I will be here to help you through this," she said in a firm, compassionate tone.

Slowly I lifted my head to meet my friend's eyes. Tears began dripping down my cheeks. The salt from them stung as they passed over the cuts on my lips. Intellectually, I was trying to formulate the words to tell Janis what I was feeling, but I began to sob. I returned her gesture, holding her briefly until the sobbing subsided. Only a few moments had passed from the time of being shame ridden to the minute I became this sobbing child to regaining my composure. Janis handed me a Kleenex. She pressed the tissue to my eyes. I could feel the swollen areas indent at the touch of her finger tips. The area was tender from the bruising. A pain shot through my nasal cavity as I blew my nose. I wadded the tissue in the palm of my hand and stuck it in my pocket as we exited the elevator.

-40-

We walked silently to the car. I was afraid to break the silence, afraid my courage would seep out and disappear through my mouth. We drove to the station without any exchange of words. I sat momentarily before exiting the car. With Janis at my side, we entered the sheriff station.

The desk sergeant looked up from his paper work as we stepped through the glass doors with a look of complacency across his face. " Can I help you?" he asked.

" Yes, we'd like to file a domestic violence report." Janis said.

" O.K. if you'll have a seat it will just be a minute. I'll get a reporting officer," he replied.

I was already sitting in a metal folding chair along the wall that faced the front desk of the station. Janis walked over from the desk and told me it would just be a minute before someone could take the report.

The sergeant picked up the phone and rang to the reporting officer on duty. An officer stepped through the door, which divided the waiting area from the rest of the station. He looked toward the desk sergeant, who motioned towards me and Janis. Approaching us, he introduced himself as Detective Hernandez.

I raised my head to meet his eyes. He stood about 5'11" with a medium muscular build. His hair was black and cut close to his head. His eyes were a soft brown color and slightly bloodshot. He had a thick black mustache that extended to the edges of his lips which were curved slightly upwards. Second thoughts were going through my mind. He extended his hand in a friendly gesture. I did not feel safe here, but it was too late to change my mind. All I could do now was leave out information that I was not comfortable divulging to the officer.

" Will you please come with me ?" he asked me.

Sensing my unease the officer suggested that Janis join me while we filled out the report. All three of us walked through the door in which the detective had entered. We made our way down the stark white hall towards the back where we entered a small room on the right. The room was brightly lit with fluorescent lights. It contained a metal desk and four folding chairs.

The officer motioned for us to take a seat in front of the desk. He positioned himself on the other side in a folding chair. He proceeded to open a drawer and pull out report form. He began by asking me general information questions. As I answered, he filled the appropriate blank spaces. Once that information was completed, Detective Hernandez began asking questions about the night of the beating.

" Were you under the influence of alcohol or any other mind altering substances?" he asked.

" I had a couple drinks early that evening," I answered.

" Did you take any drugs?"

" No," I said adamantly

" Was Larry under the influence of alcohol or any other mind altering substances?"

" Only alcohol," I responded.

" Are you certain?" he questioned.

This line of questioning was agitating me. I didn't understand what these questions had to do with beating. Finally, we began discussing the events of the abuse. Between every few questions Detective Hernandez would ask about drugs. "Had Larry or I ever done any type of drugs other than drinking?" "Was I sure Larry wasn't under the influence of any illegal substances?" My response was always the same: I completely, whole heartedly denied any such substance use.

" Why are you asking me all these questions?" I asked angrily.

" Drug and alcohol abuse are prevalent in cases of domestic violence. The officers need to know exactly who and what they are dealing with before we make an arrest. It helps ensure everyone's safety," the detective stated.

That put me a little more at ease for the remainder of the report, but I held fast to my lie. To reveal Larry's drug use would require revealing my own. The detective finished the report and gave it to me to proof read before I signed it. Scanning the report, I turned to the last page and signed it.

Janis and I stood, thanked the officer for his help and began walking out of the room.

" Wait one minute, you need a copy of the report. To check the progress of the case, call and give this file number to the front desk. Detective Furn and I will be working on this case. You can also ask to speak to one of us for an update. We will call you as soon as we have him in custody. In the meantime, stay away from him."

Thanking him again, we left the room and headed down the corridor to the exit. We stepped out into the night. The air had bit of a chill in it. I looked up into the sky, took a deep breath and gazed at the few stars I could see through the night haze. Janis stood at the driver's door waiting for me to come over to the car.

" Let's go," Janis said, sounding a bit irritated.

I walked over to the passenger door, then pulled up on the handle to let myself in. Janis had already started the engine.

" What is wrong ?" I asked.

" Why did you lie about the drugs to the cop?" Janis questioned.

" I do not feel it is any of their business. Besides, the drugs have nothing to do with the beating," I replied.

Janis looked helplessly at me and sighed. She knew there was no changing my mind on this issue. All Janis could do was pray they caught the bastard, soon.

-41-

We arrived back at the apartment around 10:00 p.m. I felt very unsure about filing the report. Had I done the right thing? What was going to happen to my relationship with Larry? Vigorously I shook my head, hoping to rattle the committee for a few moments of silence. I did not want to hear what I was thinking. I slipped into another place-- a place where everything was possible.

I imagined that the demons that plagued me fell through the opening in my ears. They stood about two inches in height. Their skin was bumpy and coarse. Their skin color was black with a red hue. Their faces had eyes the size of a pinhead, jet black in color. They projected a high pitch squeal as they hit the floor with a thump. There were six. I began to eliminate the demons. I lifted my heel above each one, lowered it on their small bodies and crushed them with my shoe. The thought of these two inch ghoulish figures trying to scamper for safe refuge, without success, made me chuckle inside.

Janis glanced over at me as I stood almost still except for raising of my right leg and grinding of my heel into the carpet. My eyes had become glazed over and the color drained from my face. Concerned, Janis tapped me on the shoulder.

Interrupted by Janis' touch I came back to reality. With the return, the weight of problems collapsed back on my shoulders. The color slowly returned to my face, but the emptiness in my eyes remained.

"Are you O.K.? " Janis asked.

" I'll be fine, " I replied as I turned the knob on my bedroom door and went inside. I closed the door behind me.

"Good night," Janis said through the door.

I could hear the befuddlement in her voice at what had just happened. She knew the only thing she could do for me now was be supportive and just be my friend. Janis headed for her room and prepared herself for bed.

I turned the lamp on next to my bed and glanced over at the window. The reflection of the light made it impossible for me to see through the darkness. I stripped off my clothes, grabbed a blanket, turned off the light and planted myself in the bean bag. The bean bag formed around every curve of my body, making me feel strangely protected. I faced the window with the phone in arm's reach.

Fear slowly crept in, overtaking my logic. Tears dripped from the corners of my eyes. Every truck that drove below my window was Larry's . Each movement and motion heard in the darkness was him. Although I lived on the second story, I knew that would not stop him. I picked up the phone and dialed. A sleepy male voice answered the other end.

"Hello," he said.

For a moment I was unable to respond to my husband's voice.

" Hello, is anyone there?" he repeated.

" Hi, Mitch, it is me. Did I wake you?" I asked.

" I just climbed into bed. What's up?"

" I fucked up, Mitch." The sobs began to catch in my throat as I tried to explain what happened the other night. The other side of the line was silent as he listened to me defend Larry's actions and question mine. He attempted to soothe me with words of encouragement that I had done the right thing.

Mitch knew me better than I knew myself, having spent the last seven years of his life with me. His consoling would only produce temporary relief for me. He loved me deeply, but he was no longer an intrinsic part of my life. I knew how Mitch felt about me. He was my safety net. I could count on Mitch to help me pick up the pieces of my shattered life. My emptiness and fear disappeared briefly while we talked. For that short time I knew someone loved me, even if I was incapable of returning that love. Exhaustion began to filter into my head and body as the conversation came to a close.

" If there is anything you need, call me." Mitch said.

" I will. Thank you for listening to me. I will be all right once the cops arrest him. Good night," I said.

I hung up the phone and I sat silently staring into the night through the open window. I picked up the phone every few minutes to check the line. Each time, there was a dial tone echoing in my ear. Why hadn't Larry called? Did he feel anything for me at all? Afraid to sleep. Afraid to dream. I fought to keep my eyelids from closing down over my eyes. I no longer had the energy to fight the exhaustion. No longer was the waking world or the dream world safe.

The following day I had an eleven o' clock shift at the restaurant. I applied my make up so as to conceal as much of the bruising as possible. I dressed in a loose fitting conservative business suit. I did not want to bring any unnecessary attention to myself. Fortunately, I could hibernate in the office most of the day. Vince would be the only person I felt an obligation to be truthful with about the beating.

I arrived at work to find Vince in the office. Before he had a chance to speak, I dove right into what had taken place. I told him I had filed a police report, but there hadn't been an arrest made, yet.

"Honey, I am so sorry this happened to you." he said with love. "Your not planning on seeing this guy again, are you?"

"No, I haven't heard from him since it happened."

"Have you gone to a doctor to make sure there was no internal damage? If not, you should go," he suggested. "Why don't you just take care of the paper work, then take the rest of the day off. Provided you go to a doctor, today."

"O.K." I said, as he stood up from the office chair and hugged me.

"Everything will be fine. I'll be on the floor if you need me. Let me know before you leave." He walked out of the office, leaving me to finish the books and find a doctor.

I was still carried under Mitch's medical insurance, so I called Brea Community Hospital emergency room to see if they would accept the carrier. I was told they would.

I left work and went straight to the emergency room. After completing the paperwork, I was immediately escorted to a room with many beds in it. Around each bed a curtain closed when it was in use. I rested on my back while I waited for the doctor.

"Well, let's see here," the doctor said, looking over my chart. He then proceeded to do some optical and reflex tests. "You have a minor concussion, but just as a precaution I am going to order some x-rays when I finish up with you. The position of your nose has been minutely altered, veering to the right. The bruising and cuts are healing as well as can be expected. I'll have a nurse take you to radiology and I'll see you when they're finished," he informed me.

Once the X-rays were developed, the doctor called me into the examination area. "Just as I suspected. There are no internal injuries. You will experience periods of dizziness due to the concussion, but other than that you're fine. If the dizziness does not subside in a couple of weeks, you should see your physician. Have a nice day."

I left Brea feeling relieved that soon the traces of beating would disappear.

The next couple of days I returned to my daily work routine, receiving a daily update from Detective Furn. It was always the same. There was still no arrest.

-43-

A loud ring abruptly woke me. I fumbled for the phone. In a sleepy voice, I answered it.

" Hi. We have to talk," the voice commanded, " but not on the phone. I will meet you at the Raddison Hotel off the 57 freeway in Brea at 6:00 p.m."

Before I could respond the dial tone was humming in my ear. Looking out the window, I realized it must be afternoon. The sun was resting high in the sky. The hands on the clock stood at 1:10 P.M. Extending my arms above my head and my legs out as far as they reached, I stretched my entire body. My stomach was turning into knots as the telephone call was beginning to sink in. With an edge of excitement and confusion, I lifted myself from the bean bag and vertically stretched my body out.

Making my way to the bathroom I sat on the toilet. As the urine flowed from my bladder, I kept replaying the phone call in my mind. Finishing my wake up procedures, I sat down at my desk and lit a cigarette, pondering whether or not to go to the Raddison. Grounding the butt of the cigarette in the ashtray, I stood up and walked over to my closet.

Moving my hands quickly through an assortment of clothes, I finally pulled out a coral cotton mini skirt with a black belt and a tight short sleeve, scoop neck black T-shirt. I draped the clothes over the chair and proceeded to take a shower. The water flowed over my body, refreshing and rejuvenating me. Turning the hot water off, I drenched myself in a five minute cold shower. Flipping my head down I squeezed the excess water from my hair. I then blindly reached for the towel that hung over the shower door. I proceeded to pat my body dry before stepping out on to the bathroom floor. With the towel wrapped turban style around my hair, I slowly approached the vanity mirror. The swelling around my eyes, cheeks and lips had vanished. The only external evidence of the beating that still existed were the thin discolored lines around my eyes, as well as a small cut on the bottom left side of my lip and the slight shift of my nasal bone.

Opening the top drawer of the vanity, I removed my makeup bag. Inspecting the contents, I took out a heavy foundation, powder, rouge and lipstick. I applied the makeup carefully and evenly over the discolored, black and blue skin. Before putting the finishing touches on, I looked deeply into the eyes that stared back from the mirror. There seemed to be no familiarity to them. I shut my eyes and I stepped away from the mirror.

I walked over to the dresser and took out a black lace Victoria's Secret bra and panty set. I slipped them on. The lace and silk against my skin felt comforting and soft. I felt sensuous in my under garments. The skirt slipped smoothly over my hips and the top fit snugly against my breasts, ending at my waist line. Provocative. I moved over to the mirrored closet door, looked over my clothing smoothing out the ridges. My lips curled upward. Even in the face of adversity, I could manage to appear appealing. I opened the closet door and took out pair of low heeled black pumps. That would be the final touch to accentuate my legs. I put the final touches on my makeup, adding mascara and a hint of lip color.

I glanced over at the clock. I still had two hours before I had to be at the hotel. I realized it had been thirty-six hours since I had given my body any healthy nutrients. I forgot do to the things that most people do routinely, and eating was one of them. I headed for the kitchen where I prepared myself a small green salad and grabbed a handful of Triscuits. Returning to my room with my meal, I sat on the bed, turned on the TV and mindlessly ate my food as I waited for time to pass.

-44-

The clock struck five thirty. It was time. Freshening up, I grabbed my purse, left the apartment and walked to my car.

The evening air was warm against my skin as the breeze blew through the open driver's side window. I drove north on the 57 freeway. I could be see the hotel from the Lambert off ramp. I exited. I pulled into the parking lot of the Raddison. I could see his truck at the far southeast corner of the lot. Before getting out of the car, I checked my hair and makeup in the rear view mirror.

He walked slowly towards my car. His fairness gave him an angelic appearance along with his soft graceful movements. He tapped on the window of my car. I reached for the handle and opened the door. He stepped back from the door, allowing me to get out of the car. He seemed uncertain how to greet me.

I stood silently before him waiting for him to respond to me. I involuntarily flinched as he stepped towards me. He kissed me. The moment I felt the warmth of his lips on my skin, all anxiety melted away. I instantly lost my ability to be objective and rational. What little common sense I had was washed away by his kiss.

" Hi. I have already registered a room for us. O.K. ?"

I responded by simply nodding my head. I followed him in through the lobby to the elevator where he pushed the fifth floor button. He inserted the card key into the door of room 512 . We stepped into the room. The door clicked shut behind me. The room contained a four person hot tub to the right and a queen size bed rested near the window. It was decorated in warm inviting colors-- sea foam green, mauve and blue. The furniture was made of medium to dark wood.

Larry had already been up to the room to prepare for my arrival. The steam rolled off the top of the jacuzzi. The surface of the water

94

was covered in a blanket of red rose petals. A single scented candle flickered, filling the room with the aroma of jasmine.

Larry immediately moved towards the hot tub, removing his clothing article by article. I watched him silently, still standing in the doorway. My heart began to beat faster at the thought of what was about to happen. Completely stripped of clothing he eased his lean muscular body into the water and allowed his body to adjust to the temperature before he completely submerged himself. He turned toward me and, with a wave of his hand, and a seductive smile, beckoned for me to join him.

Without hesitation I shed my clothing. My gaze locked on to his. I moved toward the tub. In this moment, all space and time existed. No past. No future. Only now. I lifted my right leg up to the side, then my left leg. He reached his hand from under the water and let it rest against my leg as I slid into the hot tub next to him. My nipples stood erect the moment I felt his flesh contact mine. Shivers ran through my body like an electrical jolt. He scooped me in his arms before I had an opportunity to sit, placing my delicate body on his lap. Placing his hand firmly on my face, he drew me towards him. His slightly parted lips touched mine lightly at first. Quickly the soft gentle kisses turned into passionate, unrestrained animal lust. His tongue searched the inside of my mouth. Intertwining tongues swirled around one another. My legs straddled across his lap. I could feel his hard cock rubbing against my inner thigh. His hands slipped down my neck over my shoulders, stopping at my breasts. Cupping a breast in each hand, he gently kneaded them like dough. My head fell away from his face, back arched forcing my chest closer to him. He took each nipple between his thumb and forefinger, pinching and massaging them. Moans of pleasure began escaping my lips as he expertly continued to manipulate and arouse every zone of my body. His finger tips reached my clitoris, moving them up and down in rapid movement. A warming sensation began to spread from my thighs down to my feet through my belly up to my head. My body began to convulse. I moaned with pleasure as orgasmic juices oozed from inside my body. Larry had eased inside me. His hands grasped my waist firmly as he raised me up and down. I could feel the pressure against the wall of my uterus up to my abdomen. My arms braced around his neck, we moved as one unit in ecstasy.

"Cum with me." I whispered in his ear. "I'm cumming. I'm cumming."

Together our bodies reached the ultimate height of pleasure as we melted into one being for those few moments. We embraced and kissed. He lifted me from the jacuzzi. Held in his arms, he carried me to the bed and gently laid me down. My eyes closed, but I could feel him staring at me as I lay exposed on the bed.

-45-

He began to move his hands over the bruises on my legs and face, pressing his lips against each wound. I remained completely still. Climbing on to the bed, he laid next to me, rested his head on my chest, and began to weep. I cradled him in my arms. He wept like a child full of remorse. His tears melted away any anger I had left towards him.

Looking into my eyes he stammered out, "I'm so sorry!"

"Why did you do it. Why did you hurt me?" I asked.

"I felt so rejected and angry when you told me to get out of the car. It was like I became possessed by something I was unable to control. I promise you it will never happen again."

His words penetrated my heart. I felt only love and compassion for this man, this child. I continued to listen.

"I do not want to lose you. If the cops catch me and put me in jail I will not be able to hold you in my arms, make love to you and share my life with you. Please, I beg of you, drop the charges. We can start over again."

" I think you need help, professional help."

" I don't need help, I'm not crazy. What I need is a second chance to prove my love to you. Will you give me that?"

"Yes, I will go down to the station tomorrow and drop the charges."

The intensity of his sobbing increased as he thanked me for loving him and giving him his freedom. We held each other tightly as we drifted into the world of dreams.

I opened my tired eyes, confused by the strange bed that I lay in. Sweat dripping from my brow. Short erratic breaths. My breathing slowly became regular as I realized I was in a hotel room with Larry. I could feel the warmth of his breath on my neck as he slept peacefully beside me. I did not want to close my eyes for fear of what I might see. Unable to fight the weariness any longer, however, I drifted into a restful sleep.

-46-

We awoke late the following morning. We held each other briefly before rising out of bed. We each gathered up our clothes from the previous night. I pulled a pair of shorts and a T-shirt from my purse and put them on. Larry threw on last night's attire. Taking one final look around the room to ensure we had all our belongings, we headed for the door. Before exiting the room, Larry pulled me close to him, tilted my head upwards and kissed me. He wrapped his arms around my waist and bent his head down so his mouth was near my ear.

"After you drop the charges, come over to my house and we will celebrate. I Love you, Louise, never forget that," he whispered.

He released me from his embrace. We left the hotel. Larry waved to me as he pulled out of the Raddison parking lot.

I followed suit. I headed north on the 57 Freeway towards the Walnut sheriff station. I pulled into the station parking lot. I sat in my car rehearsing what I would say, before going inside. When I entered the building, I immediately approached the desk sergeant.

"Excuse me, I filed assault charges and I would like to drop them."

"Do you have the file number?" the desk sergeant asked.

I opened my purse, pulled out the paper work and gave it to the sergeant.

"If you'll have a seat the detective on the case will be right with you."

My heart raced as I waited in the cold metal chair for the detective. Detective Furn peered through the office door and summoned me to accompany him to his office.

"I understand you want to drop the charges against Mister Jennings. Can you tell me why?"

"Well, I just don't want to press charges, that's all," I said.

"Has he threatened you in any way to encourage this change of heart?" Detective Furn asked.

"No, it was completely my decision."

"You do understand we can not protect you if you drop these charges," he said.

"I don't need protection. I just want this nightmare to be over, O.K."

"O.K., here is our number. If there is anything I or my partner Detective Hernandez can do for you, please do not hesitate to call."

As I stood to leave I thanked the detective for his understanding. I stood outside the office door and, in doing so, I overheard the detectives talking.

Detective Furn and Hernandez waited for me to exit before they spoke.

"She'll be back." Furn stated.

"I hope so. I want this guy off the streets. This guy has been a thorn in our side for too long. I don't want to see her name on the homicide sheet."

"It's just a matter of time before we have some solid evidence to arrest this guy. He is a time bomb waiting to explode."

"You're right. Let's just stick close to this girl."

"All right."

I moved away from the door, left the building and headed for Larry's.

I arrived at Larry's around 2:00 p.m. Robby, his roommate for the time being, answered the door. Robby was medium height, medium build. His weight was proportionate to his size. His hair was short, thick and wavy, and his face was scarred from pubescent acne problems. If one word could describe Robby it was smarmy.

" Is Larry here?" I asked.

" Have you dropped the charges?" he questioned before letting me in.

" Yeah, everything is cool."

With that cleared up he invited me in. " He's upstairs."

I ran upstairs to the master bedroom. I found Larry lying on his back, his arms folded beneath his head. He opened his eyes at the sound of my footsteps. I jumped on the bed beside him and feverishly kissed his face.

"I guess since you're here that means the charges have been dropped," he said with calm assurance.

I nodded as I continued my playful kitten demeanor.

"Why don't you draw us a couple of lines. It 's in the usual place," he said.

"O.K." Within seconds I was up and had the blade in hand and was drawing a couple of big ones. The sound of inhalation rung in my ears as he got up and walked over to where I was seated. He bent over and whiffed up his line. He dropped the tooter on the mirror and placed his hands on my shoulders. Massaging and caressing my back and shoulders, he suggested we call some friends and take a drive to Laguna Beach that evening.

" That would be fun," I said.

We made love all afternoon. I had never experienced ecstasy and with such an intense passion with any man to the magnitude I did with Larry. He could bring me to multiple orgasms in one session. It wasn't merely a pelvic orgasm it was a body, mind and spirit eruption. During our sexual interludes, everything was right with the world and our relationship. That was the one plane we connected completely on.

Dusk was starting to overtake the sunlight when we finished. Soon our friends would be arriving. We quickly showered together and dressed in casual clothes. I packed a couple of blankets and some snacks for the beach. We would stop on the way to purchase some spirits. Larry had taken up the hobby of RC cars. Larry grabbed his two favorite cars and some parts and placed them with the things I had packed. The doorbell rang. While Larry answered the door, I grabbed the bag and headed downstairs.

Everyone was in good spirits when they arrived at Larry's house. We all partook in a little party favors, then we were ready to leave. Larry, Robby, and I rode in his truck. The others rode with Darin in his car. Larry followed closely behind Darin as we made our way south on the 405 freeway towards Laguna. Once we exited the freeway, we stopped at a local liquor store and bought some drinks. By the time we arrived at Laguna Beach it was dark outside. The beach was vacant. We parked the cars, grabbed the firewood, the booze, and the bag and walked to the sand.

After lighting a large bonfire, the guys immediately began running their RC cars in the sand. I was the only girl. I left the boys to play with their toys. I walked over to the jetty, and climbed out onto the rocks. I found a comfortable place to enjoy the sound of the sea breaking against the rocks, the sea mist washing over me and watching the water kiss the sand with reckless abandon. The water had always been a tranquil place for me to find refuge from life. Nothing could hurt me here and all my problems were washed away with the constant movement of the tide, even if it was only for awhile. The moon was full and its light shimmered on the surface of the water. The white wash seemed to boil as it splashed on the rocks. I sensed him standing behind me on the rocks. He embraced me from behind.

" Are you all right?" he asked.

" I'm fine, just enjoying the moment," I responded.

" I have a drink for you. Here. We'll be leaving soon. I'll come get you," he said.

" Thanks for the drink. See you in a bit," I answered.

A couple of hours passed when I noticed him packing up and putting out the bonfire. I left my seaside sanctuary and joined everyone else. We put the stuff in the truck and left.

-47-

I began spending every spare moment with Larry. The days turned into weeks. Although he had not raised a hand to me since the incident last month, our relationship was rocky. Like a brown recluse spider, he had bitten my soul and I was oblivious to the wound. I would require a complete reconstruction. His behavior had become erratic. One minute he was warm and loving, the next he would be screaming at me for some reason I was unable to identify. I continued to be pulled in closer to the circle, the danger.

Since I wasn't spending much time at my apartment, we decided I should move in with Larry. I drove home one hot July afternoon to tell Janis and Carol I would be moving. I arrived at the apartment to find Janis at home.

" Hi. How are you? " I asked.

Janis immediately sensed my uneasiness.

" I'm fine. What's up? Is something bothering you?" she asked.

" Yes and no. I wanted to tell you I'm moving in with Larry."

Janis was stunned.

" Why? You know what's going to happen. You're going to be his captive. You will lose your job and drop out of school. He wants to have complete control over you. Please don't make this mistake," she said.

" Janis, everything will be fine. He loves me and I love him. I've worked to hard towards my degree, I'm not going to drop out with only one year to go. Work will always be there. I'm sorry if this is an inconvenience for you and Carol, but I have to do this for me. I'll go down to the office and give a thirty day notice if you want me to. Janis, I know you don't understand, but I know what I'm doing." Janis had a far better understanding of the situation than I could have possibly dreamed. I knew nothing.

" I worry about you. You've changed so much over the last couple of months. I wish I had the same faith you do that you'll be all right. I'll talk to Carol about whether or not to give up the apartment. If we decide to leave, I'll let the office know. When are you planning to move?"

" I'll start moving my stuff this week. Thank you for everything."

I wrapped my arms around Janis. We held each other for a moment. Tears streamed down from our eyes as we said good bye. Janis had a tone of finality in her words of good bye.

Darin, Larry and I spent the week moving my belongings to Larry's. By the last week of July I had left my keys at the office and now had a new residence. My belongings occupied the small bedroom adjacent to Larry's room, but my being occupied his room.

Within a week of moving into Larry's, my life turned to complete chaos and insanity.

-48-

I was dressed in a pair of black shorts and a work shirt. I pulled my now shoulder length hair into a pony tail. I walked through the kitchen to the garage to say good bye to Larry before I went to work. It was ten o' clock in the morning and he was sitting behind the metal desk in the corner of the garage doing a line.

"I have to go. I'll see you around four. " I bent over to kiss him. He grabbed my arm and held it tightly. I tried to pull away, but his grip only tightened. He had a look of desperation on his face as he stared at me. "I have to go to work, let me go!"

"You're going to call work and quit. Now!" he ordered.

"What are you talking about? I can't call work and just quit. That would not be cool."

"If you do not call right now, I guarantee people are going to be hurt. I'll start with your family. Don't you understand? Your boss is trying to get me busted." He just kept rattling off people in my life who were supposedly out to destroy him. He was talking nonsense. I tried to tell him that whatever was going on in his mind would go away once he got some sleep, but he was unrelenting about my family if I did not do what he said. I had so little self worth, self respect, self love left by this time, that I was unable to summon the courage to stand up to this ludicrous behavior.

I made the phone call and never went back to work for the remainder of our relationship. He forced me to make phone calls to the few friends I had left and tell them I did not want to have anything to do with them. A little piece of me seemed to wither away with each call, with each lie. But nothing was stronger than

102

the fear I had of this man, of what he would do to the people I loved. I was not willing to find out what lengths he would go to.

Once I had succumbed to his will, the next couple of days were uneventful.

There was a buzz in the inner circle that someone in the outside circle was an informant. Although mere speculation, intuitively I knew it was someone in the inner circle. Those outside of it were simply pawns of the system.

Darin had recently acquired a girlfriend, Michelle. Michelle was a love child. PCP, acid, love, peace, the whole nine yards. She seemed to float when she walked. Long straight blonde hair. A waif like figure. Soft green eyes that expressed a gentleness in her soul. She dressed in loose, second hand clothes that made her appear thinner than she was. She partook in the pink, but PCP was her love. Out of curiosity I questioned her about the effects of PCP. She said it made the whole world beautiful when she looked through the eyes of this drug induced state. I was always to fearful to experiment with it, but soon I would know first hand the effects of PCP.

Michelle and I quickly became friends. I was starved for female companionship since I had discontinued all contact with my old friends. Michelle filled that hunger. Darin practically lived with us, so when Michelle appeared they were a package.

Robby was still renting one of the downstairs bedrooms. He was a dope fiend like the rest of us. He ingratiated himself in our lives, trying penetrate the circle, but the links were welded tight. When I looked into his dark brown eyes, I experienced a feeling of distrust. He did have a gift for upholstery, which is what he did for a living when he chose to work.

In the midst of my illusion, I sunk deeper into the darkness turning it into my reality.

I found that Larry twisted and turned every word I spoke inside out so as it would appear I was somehow defying him or the group. With every action that moved me he would scrutinize and question my loyalty. With each abusive act, mental and/or physical, a strip of my self-worth would be removed and in its place terror danced.

-50-

Rick was expected to arrive soon. Larry, Darin, Michelle, Robby and I waited patiently in Larry's garage. We played darts and drank beer. Michelle had just smoked a Kool. She was gently swaying in the corner to the beat of her own drummer.

Rick arrived around six o clock that evening. We quickly moved the party indoors, all waiting for our first line of the day.

"I have the stuff, but first I need to let you know what is going on. I have reason to believe we're--or should I say you, Larry--are under investigation. Bottom line is, we all need to be especially careful. I think the cops are getting their information from an inside source, but I have no idea who. Keep an eye on your buyers. Here is a little tip. Before you sell to anyone, ask them if they are a cop or an informant. Only take a yes/no answer. If they answer no and they are a cop, any information that is gathered is obtained illegally and therefore inadmissible." Rick spoke in a commanding authoritative tone, "If you just do what I say, everything will be fine, but we need to find the weak link."

Rick effectively planted the seeds of distrust and fear.

I looked quizzically at the others. I could feel their eyes staring at me. I knew because of the police report I had filed against Larry and my arrest in April they were questioning my loyalty in their minds. Each of us only knew what was in our individual hearts, and I knew my loyalty to Rick and Larry would not waver, at least to the extreme the others were speculating it did. An uneasiness rose in the air of the living room that night. It would force each of us to turn on one another, except for the one who kept a foot on each side of the law. Paranoia would seep slowly in and run deep in Larry's mind at the broadcast of Rick's warning. No one spoke about what thoughts entered their mind at that moment. Rick allowed what he had said to absorb and process into our thoughts.

I turned my eyes back to Rick. I looked at him pleadingly to say something, to ease the moment and bring some levity back into our hearts.

He looked sympathetically back, winked at me and with a radiant smile forming at his lips he broke the silence. "Let's party. I realized I just laid a heavy load on you guys, but like I said, if you follow my suggestions everything thing will be as it is supposed to be." With that, he pulled out a baggy full of the pink and drew up six monster lines.

The skepticism and tension was no longer blatantly at the surface our minds, but if I listened close enough, it was the underlying theme of our discussions.

Most had returned to the garage. Rick remained seated in the living room talking to Larry and taking care of business. When Larry walked upstairs to put away the meth, I moved closer to Rick so that I could talk to him discretely.

"Rick, I feel like everyone thinks it's me, even Larry. Rick, you have to know that whatever is going on with the cops I have nothing to with it. I love Larry and you, I would never rat on anyone, no matter what." My pulse quicked and my tongue became thick as I tried to defend actions I never perpetrated. I was reaching out for his assurance and friendship at that moment.

He slipped his strong arm around my shoulder in a gentle loving manner and looked directly into my fearful eyes. " Louise, this is a tough time right now. I know you're cool, but what you don't realize is that, in this business, women are the weak link because they are ruled by their emotions. So in order to curb any doubts in the mind of the others, never let them see you cry and never, never act emotionally irrational. I trust you and I love you, we are friends. I just have to let this run its course, you'll be fine. I will always be available when you need me."

Whatever I heard in that dialogue made me feel safe, but at that moment a barrier the size of the Great Wall of China was constructed around my heart, and dams were built in my tear ducts. We chatted idly for a few more moments until Larry descended the stairs.

Rick stood up. "Well, I'd better run, you guys should go out and have some fun tonight. It would do you good." Shaking Larry's hand and giving me one of his hearty Rick hugs, he said, "I'll see you soon."

That night Darin, Michelle, Larry and I decided to get a suite at the Radisson, taking our booze and drugs on the road and leaving Robby at home.

We registered in my name because I was the only one with a credit card for the phone, but Larry paid cash for the room. The suite had a large living area and a hot tub that would comfortably fit six. We felt much more at ease since we left Larry's, but pondered the questions between us on who the traitor might be.

We started tweaking hard, which for me sometimes opened my mind to other realms and possibilities. I went through the drawers of the night stand and found The Teachings of Buddha where the King James Bible was normally placed. That would be my first introduction to eastern philosophy and also a godsend when my life grew more turbulent. I began to read some of the passages out loud.

"Resentment cannot be satisfied by resentment; it can only be removed by forgetting it."

"Right behavior means not to destroy any life, not to steal, or not commit adultery."

I looked up from the book and noticed they were looking at me attentively. Larry made a motion with his hand to continue.

"There are fires of greed, fires of anger, fires of foolishness.......suffering agony. Everywhere these fires are raging. They not only burn the self, but also cause others to suffer......From the wounds that are caused by these fires there issues a pus that infects and poisons those who approach it...."

Larry looked at me quizzically and in childlike voice asked, "What does that mean?"

I could explain it to him only as I perceived it. I handed him the book to read, which he immediately rejected. This night of new found awareness, I came to realize Larry was basically illiterate, reading and writing at a second grade level. I had never put it together before now. He always had someone else write notes, bills or letters and acted like he was to busy to pick up a simple mortgage statement and read. I often had to read something and tell him what it said. Larry was raised under the hand of an alcoholic, physically violent father. Then one day his father, left and Larry was left in the care of his mother and her unexpressed emotions. Then when Larry was a teenager his only brother committed suicide in Larry's room. More than ever I wanted to rescue this man. Not only was he deprived of a happy childhood , but he was robbed of an education from our wonderful public school system. At least, that is how I justified staying, in mind. I noticed as I read that this was the first time since that meeting in the bar, that I saw a sparkle in his blue eyes.

It was an evening of which the magic still brings a smile to my lips. Partying, spiritual readings, discussion and making love under the stars on the balcony of our room, while Michelle and Darin relaxed in the hot tub and played doctor.

The teachings reached out to a part of my soul that was unscathed by my reckless past, a place that was full of wonderment and God. The words shed light on my present, made sense of my past and gave me hope for the future. They spoke directly to my spirit.

As we returned home the following day, the distrust, secrecy, and paranoia Rick had imbedded remained in the house.

-52-

Still running on fuel from the evening before, I busied myself around the house, reorganizing closets, doing laundry, going through drawers looking for anything that would give some insight into what was going on around us.

Larry found me in my room working on my computer and proceeded to rant and rave about something being moved or gone through.

"I don't have any idea what you're talking about, you probably just misplaced it," I countered.

He grabbed my arm, pulled me from the chair and slapped me. I had long since learned not to try to fight him physically, but verbally I attempted to pulverize him. That only made it worse. No tears would fall from my eyes when he left me crumbled on the floor. There was plenty of room in that empty hole inside of me for the tears to fall, unspoken and unseen. I sat there in a daze, trying to clear my head of the thick fog.

Michelle handed me a cigarette. It was menthol, but it had left an unknown taste in my mouth. The usual buzz of people coming and going continued throughout the day into the late evening, as I became more and more detached from reality.

"You need to eat something, I'll make you some eggs," Larry said as looked through the refrigerator and pulled out the milk and eggs.

I sat at the kitchen table waiting for my first meal in several days. The light was so bright it made me squint. He placed a plate of eggs and a glass of milk in front of me.

"Make sure you eat it all," Darin said as he sat next to me, encouraging me to finish every last morsel. I cleaned my plate without uttering a word and pushed it away.

"O.K. you can get up now. Why don't you go lay down in the extra room down here" Larry suggested as he cleared my plate from the table.

I rose without a thought in my head, but my body moved towards the bedroom. I could hear Rick and Larry talking somewhere in the distance, although I had not seen Rick that day. I lay down, not knowing why, just going through the motions.

All of a sudden I felt Larry's fist pounding on my body, but I could not see him. My screams were deafening to my ears. I moved my body to protect myself from my unseen assailant. I could hold back the tears no longer as they spilled from my eyes. I lifted my head slightly and saw Larry, Rick, the Fly, who was the manufacturer of "the pink", and Darin standing against the wall five feet away from the bed. No one was near me. "Please make it stop, you didn't tell me it would be like this," I heard Larry plead.

"We have to do this. We have to find out if she'll break," Rick said as they looked on.

I felt every blow, every kick, and every ounce of pain of my hallucination. When it stopped, I lay there and wept uncontrollably until Larry ordered me to get up. I did not want to move, but my body responded without my permission. For what seemed like days I lost complete control of my movements and my mind.

Larry would bark commands at me and I would follow the orders, I tried to retaliate by enforcing my will, but it didn't work. I was ordered to walk up the stairs. The dogs lay quietly at the bottom. As I moved towards them, their shape changed to that of pigs. I wanted to run, but couldn't. As Larry stood behind me, it felt like a knife was pushed into my lower back. Warm blood trickled down my spine. He yelled, "Stop" when I reached the landing. My feet might as well have been buried in cement at the moment he barked the order. I could not move. He slid by me. Now he was facing me, and telling me I was the one who informed the police, that I was the one who was the traitor. I helplessly shook my head in denial while fighting back the tears. He ran the tip of a double edged knife down my throat, breaking the skin, while hurling more accusations at me. Occasionally he would raise his hand. The blade moved along my jaw line and eventually it felt as if my entire neck was covered in blood. My body bruised. My mind lost. My spirit dead. We reached his room. He handed me a paper and pen. "Write what I tell you," he said.

"I am an informant. I, Louise, am a narc. Sign it."

I looked down at my hand it moved across the paper writing what he said. I tried to convince him this wasn't true.

He removed his sword from its sheath and placed it with the blade facing upwards the tip pointing at his heart. Tears started to roll down his face. His words were unclear except that he no longer wanted to live.

I pleaded with him not to take his life. I would die before I let that happen. Then he turned the sword tip towards me and told me to get out of his house.

"No, I can't leave, please," I whined. The fear of what was out there outweighed the destruction of what was taking place within the walls.

He stood above me, his body appearing larger and evil. I cowered beneath him. He pushed me towards the bedroom door and down the stairs. "Get out!" he screeched.

I found myself standing outside the front door, not knowing what day it was or where I was going. I had only the clothes on my back. The sky was solid gray with a chill in the air, even though it was August. Rebel and Misty, Larry's two pit bulls, stood at my feet. I looked across the cul-de-sac and down the street. I began moving south, staying within the confines of the houses.

The dogs followed me as I walked. I could hear Larry call for his dogs. Misty returned, but Rebel continued to stay right next to my feet. I was operating purely on instinct, and some subconscious inner guidance. I made a left on the first street, then the next quick left. I was walking up a hill. I knew I had to keep moving. "Don't look back, keep moving upward," echoed in my head, so I continued up the hill.

"Rebel, come here. Rebel come here, boy," I heard Robby call.

I stopped. I looked to see Robby stopped in his car. Rebel looked up at me. He seemed confused, moved a couple of steps closer to the car with each call of his name. Then Rebel would run back to me. I knelt down, rubbed his ears and whispered "Go on home, baby, go home." He ran to the car and Robby drove away. I was on my own.

I made a turn here and there but the progression continued to move upwards. I finally found myself standing at the top of a street looking between two houses on the hill, being mystically pulled to the dirt mound behind them. It appeared that no one was home. I climbed between the houses. I was standing alone on a hill that overlooked the south end of town, including Larry's house. I bent my head down to the earth and a cross stood at my feet. It was made of two small branches and stood about a foot and a half to two feet high. At that moment a wave of peace shot through my body along with the realization that I would be all right and I was not alone. There was someone, something in the universe, whether it was on earth or not I did not know, but I was protected. I stood there and allowed this feeling to flood my body. I left the hill, never to find that place again, but the awareness would remain with me forever.

I walked back towards Larry's house. As I got closer, the feeling of safety was evaporating. I looked to the heavens and asked, " Am I ever going to come down from this? Please help me. God, please help."

I made my way back to Larry's house, still in awe of the unexplainable experience, and in fear of his rage. He let me back in. Not only was my mind operating from an altered state, my body was completely deprived of healthy nourishment.

I walked through the entryway into the living room. The bronze panther statue was perched elegantly, in a stalking stance, on the twenty year-old box television. The eyes were made of fiery ruby gems that glimmered in the darkness. As I passed in front of the panther the eyes followed me across the dimly lit room.

Paranoia beset my body. I turned my head quickly to catch the movement of the panther's eyes and caught a brief glimpse of movement. I could feel the eyes burning into my back. Were there mini-cameras stalking my every move? Who would be behind such an elaborate device? The Sheriff? The Fly? I had fallen over the cliff of sanity and was dangling by an unseen force.

I moved through the dining room to the sliding glass door and slid it open. The others, Darin, Michelle, Rick and Robby, were seated outside. Larry followed me. The sun had evaporated the cloud cover of the morning. It's heat made me sweat. Was it still the same day, I asked myself, as I looked up into the blue sky. Beams of red and green light shot through the sky, coming from the helicopter that hovered above the house in an attempt to line up their possible target, Larry. With a misplaced since of loyalty, I protected his body with mine, acting as human shield. As he moved from one place to another in the back yard, I became his shadow and protector. No harm would come to me, and if it did I would die. The mental mind-fucking was being taken to its extremes, and I was the laboratory rat.

Sleep had finally found me. I opened my eyes. I looked around, not knowing how or when I arrived in Larry's bed, or how long I had been there. I was waking alone, fully clothed. No light came through the window. "It must be night, or am I still hallucinating?" I thought. The house sounded empty. "Larry, Robby, Darin anyone here?" I yelled out. No one answered. I felt like Rip Van Wrinkle coming out of a hundred year sleep. What had happened before my head hit the pillow? I had the vivid memories, but I questioned them. I ran to the mirror to look for lacerations some physical sign of what had transpired, but there where none. Only a couple of bruises on my legs and arms, but it was hard to say when they sprouted on my flesh. I locked the memories away in my internal basement. For now, I was content to no longer feel out of control, but my fears grew.

No one was home, but the garage door was open. I knew the house would not remain empty for long. I stood in the open doorway between the kitchen and the garage for a moment, when Rick appeared.

"I came by earlier. I went upstairs and tried to wake you, but you wouldn't budge." His eyes twinkled as he talked to me. His voice gave me no indication that anything out of the ordinary had taken place lately, so I kept the events to myself, even though I was certain he was the instigator of the journey.

I just continued to stare at him for a few minutes, letting my gut talk to me. "It is like he knows when he needs to be here. For some reason I know I am safe with this man. Who is he?" I stared into his eyes and I sensed he had a profound respect for me, due to my actions and reactions to the events that previously been played out. He knew, they all knew, Larry's propensity for paranoia and his irrational behavior would always be directed at me regardless of my obvious loyalty to him and the others. I sensed that the battery of test Rick had felt compelled to administer to me, had appeased any doubt in his and the others minds.

" Are you O.K.?"

"Oh yeah. I'm fine. Sorry, I just woke up. I'm still a little spacey. Have you seen any of the gang?" I asked as we stood facing each other in the kitchen.

"I found this note earlier, " he said, handing, me a piece of paper from his pocket. "Babe, didn't want to wake you, be back soon. Luv Larry.

"Well, I have to run. I just wanted to come by and check on things. Tell Larry I'll be by later." With a friendly kiss on the cheek, he left me standing in my thoughts.

-53-

Larry returned late that evening. He walked through the garage then immediately closed it. I was still in the kitchen sitting at the table in the dark, with my chin propped up in my hands, thinking. Without a word, he began frantically walking through the house, locking all the doors and windows to the outside world.

" What are you doing?" I asked from the kitchen.

"Someone's out to get me. The cops are watching the house. Come look," he said as he walked into Robby's room, to the window that faced the street. He pulled the curtain aside just enough to have a clear view of the office building across the boulevard.

I followed behind curiously, wondering what the hell he was talking about. "Let me see " I looked. I saw the second story windows that faced the house. The lights were on. There appeared to be some kind of activity going on. I could see shadows moving across the blinds that were partially open. "It is probably just the cleaning crew," I said. I let the curtain drop back across the window.

"No, it's not. Not on a Sunday at this hour. Rick warned us. I'm telling you, someone is trying to get me busted," he said, looking at me wide-eyed and scared. "We can't leave the house for awhile."

" What do you mean we can't leave the house? For how long?"

I couldn't believe the implication of what he was saying.

"Please, I just need you to stick by me on this," he said as he took my hands, pleading for my allegiance.

"All right," I said.

For six days, I stayed confined to the house with Larry, never stepping outside. The drapes were all drawn shut even though it was August, the hottest time of the year. I was caged inside the walls.

People would come in, but we never left. Everyone who entered was questioned about any association with the police or whether they had been arrested or pulled over. The questions were rarely direct. Through a series of mental manipulation games, he scrutinized and dehumanized each of our friends. Sometimes they were not permitted to leave the house until he had coerced the answer he wanted to hear. Forget about what the truth was, or that this investigation was the direct result of his behavior on the streets. Heaven forbid Larry take responsibility himself. He had this ability to instill fear in most people on the outside circle of our world. The people he was interrogating were the same ones that brought us cigarettes and beer while we were locked up. Michelle and Darin remained behind the doors with us the first few days until Larry ran them out of the house, with his paranoid, schizophrenic, unpredictable behavior. Darin was still never far away.

Every night, I would look out the window at the building across the street. It was always active. I quickly bought into the theory that Larry was being investigated. Not only was he a dope dealer, he was a menace to society. He drove the city streets erratically, endangering anyone who was driving on them. He had a complete disregard for human life, so it seemed like the natural progression of things that the police would latch onto anything that would help them get him off the streets and put him away.

I found myself peering out the sliding glass door one day at three officers standing on the perimeter of the property, waiting in the empty field for Larry to come out. I yearned to feel the sun on my skin, the wind blow through my hair, to breath the smoggy California air. Too fearful to leave, I sat and poured over the Teachings of Buddha, trying absorb something to cling to in this time of insanity and uncertainty.

The evening of the day Darin and Michelle left, I heard shouting coming from another area of the house. Robby had come home from work about fifteen minutes before the shouting started. Robby had continued his daily routine despite Larry's insistence that he and I stay in the house. I followed the sound of the yelling towards kitchen. I stopped abruptly at the doorway to the kitchen and watched the scene in dismay.

"Robby, I suggest you finish the upholstery work on my truck by tomorrow!" Larry said with his voice raised.

"Dude, I'll get to it when I get a chance. Man, I just walked in the door, give me a break," Robby responded. As he turned to walk out of the kitchen Larry forcefully shoved Robby into the stove. "Hey, what the hell are you doing?" Robby said in retaliation as he tried to put some distance between himself and Larry.

"Nobody works me like that! Get the hell out of my house, get the hell out, now! " Larry screamed.

Robby began walking towards my direction in order to leave the kitchen. "O.K. let me grab my wallet and some clothes, " Robby said. I stepped back from the doorway as Robby passed me and walked down the hall. I felt invisible as Larry lunged passed me at Robby.

I turned and followed quickly behind Larry, "Larry, let him get his wallet. He said he would leave," I pleaded to Larry , but my pleas went unheard. Larry reached Robby moments after his departure from the kitchen. From behind, Larry shoved him into the bathroom, and while Robby was attempting to regain his balance, Larry pulled out his knife. With his hand wrapped around the blunt end, of the handle, he slammed his fist into Robby's face, a number of times, while screaming, "Get out of my house!"

My mouth hung open in silence as I watched. Blood was streaming down Robby's face. It appeared to be coming from his mouth. Robby tried to block the blows, but he had not regained his balance from the initial shove into the bathroom. "O.K., O.K. I'll go, " he whimpered under his breath.

From somewhere inside I screamed, "Larry, stop it!" Abruptly Larry's hand stopped in mid air and he said, "Get out before I change my mind."

Robby darted past me and out the front door. I heard his tires screech against the pavement as he pulled away from the house. I looked at Larry in disbelief as he said, "Nobody tries to play me for a fool. Remember that Louise." Simultaneously he cleaned the knife and slipped it back in its sheath that was attached to his belt. Then he turned and left me standing there in silence.

I had already become privy to the truth of Larry's erratic, unjustified episodes. Everyday Larry would find a reason to project his rage on me. He turned on me like a wild dog that was forced in a cage. I would run up the stairs each time the beast exposed itself, but he always followed me. Larry punched me in the gut when I told him I was pregnant. I miscarried shortly thereafter. He would pin me into a corner and smash my head against a wall, or hold me securely by the shoulders and, with all his weight, crush my feet beneath his shoes. My three middle toes on each foot were broken and never given a chance to heal before the next assault. Somehow, my spirit would soar high above my body while I was being beaten. I would look down at my body and watch, never feeling the pain of the attack. I no longer knew how to cry. It hurt when I walked most of the time, but I soon adjusted and absorbed it as part of my life. There was always a bright light that flashed before my eyes as my head collided with a wall. I was approaching the brink of madness. The internal emotional cancer was a malignant tumor on my soul, slowly spreading.

The sheriffs no longer seemed to be lurking around, yet we did not dare go outside. I don't know which was worse, the unsolicited PCP trip, or being locked up like a laboratory specimen, waiting. It was as if I had been pulled up from the side of the cliff, only to keep one foot hanging over the edge and knowing that at any given moment, I could fall into the dark abyss below, never to return.

We were out of food, except a for lonely jar of generic Spaghetti sauce. I had lost close to ten pounds, since the day I moved in with Larry. I did not need to lose anymore. I stood in front of the open refrigerator, hoping something would materialize, or I'd be eating dog food covered in a rich flavorful tomato sauce. Amazingly enough, my request for food was answered.

I heard the front door close, and wondered what was going on. Then I heard Rick's voice float through the room. I ran to the living room and threw my arms around him. He was the only man Larry allowed me to be outwardly affectionate towards.

"I'm so happy to see you!" I said with as much glee as a prisoner could. "How are you? Where have you been? Man, I'm climbing the walls being cooped up in here."

"Everything is fine, there haven't been any new developments in finding out who is spilling the beans. I had a feeling I needed to see how you two were weathering the situation." He spoke to me in a gentle, brotherly voice as he walked into the kitchen and pulled open the fridge. "Well, looks like I showed up just in time. The cupboards are pretty bare."

The only thing inside the pantry was a bag of dog food. The dogs were always first priority with Larry.

Talking directly to Larry, who had followed him into the kitchen, Rick said, "Why don't I take Louise to the grocery store and buy you two some food? She needs to get out of the house. Not only is she wasting away physically, but she seems despondent."

Larry nodded his head in approval.

My face must have immediately lit up and Rick looked in my direction with a smile from ear to ear and winked at me. It was as if to say, "Hey kid, I told you I'd be here when you needed me. I'm not going to let you waste away." I was so excited I ran upstairs, threw on a pair of shorts and T-shirt, and in a matter of minutes we were on our way. Larry stayed behind.

We laughed and talked. I wanted to know how his timing was always so appropriate. How he always arrived to shed some light and pull me out of the darkness. His response was always the same. "I just have that ability to know when and where I'm needed." Then he'd always say with a chuckle "I'm your angel."

"Well, whatever or whoever you are, I am so grateful for your help and for being my friend. I love you for being you. Thank you," I said, teary eyed with gratitude as we drove to the store.

He smiled at me sheepishly and turned the conversation to a lighter subject.

I prolonged the shopping for as long as possible. With every breath of outdoor air I was thankful, for every stranger who looked upon me with judgment I was thankful, with every passerby that smiled my direction I was thankful, to be squinting in the fluorescent lights of the store I was thankful. I was thankful to be free, even if that freedom would be short lived.

Rick was getting ready to leave after the groceries had been unloaded, but before he departed he assured us that it was O.K. to go out and about as long as we laid low on the meth scene. "I realize you have run out of stuff. In a week or two when everything is cooled down it will be O.K. to start making some money and I'll bring you over a new supply. Until then, do not do any dealing," he warned as he headed out the door.

We never questioned Rick. We just believed his words were like gospel. Maybe we could go hang out somewhere, I said to myself.

Late that evening we returned home after filling our empty bellies with pizza and beer, I lay in bed pondering who Rick was. Where did he come from? I knew there was more to him and his past than would be revealed at this point, but I believed strongly that if I trusted him and followed his suggestions, I would be safe. My gut and my heart both echoed that sentiment loudly in my mind. I was finally learning to listen and trust my inner voice

-54-

The day was sweltering as we drove in silence to Pomona to the home of a friend of Darin's. The prior situation with the police appeared to be over and no further activity was apparent to us, Darin and some sense of normalcy returned. It was dusk when we pulled up in front of the house, where a few people were buzzing around in the yard. When we entered the house, marijuana assaulted my nostrils. The atmosphere was filled with laughter, induced from the effects of the THC. I greeted the few people I knew and accepted the offering of a beer. There were a couple people in the living room strumming away on acoustical guitars. I found myself a comfortable space on the couch where I could enjoy my drink and the music.

Larry and Darin went directly to one of the bedrooms upon entering the house. They stayed sequestered there for the next hour, playing video games and taking tokes off the bong.

I had become enthralled with the sound of the cords floating through the room when Larry appeared.

"Do you want to get a couple hits of acid?" he asked.

"Sure, what kind is it?" I questioned.

"Micro dot. Twenty dollars for three hits," he said.

"O.K." I replied.

The two times I had tried acid, my trips had been filled with laughter and enlightening hallucinations, but in the back of mind I held on to an ounce of fear. "What if I have a bad trip?" Nonetheless, I didn't allow that to stop me.

I finished my beer, and we said our good byes and headed out the door.

Once we had arrived at Larry's house, Darin, Larry and I immediately took our hits. Within a half an hour we were all beginning to feel the effect of the chemicals on our brain.

Larry crawled up in the rafters of the garage and came across some type of game he was unaware that he had. The game consisted of 5 by 7 cards with animated pictures of faces and names on them. When he returned from the garage, he walked into the dining room and dropped the cards on to the table. Darin and I looked quizzically at Larry, waiting for an explanation.

"Who do you think put these up in the rafters, and what do you think they mean?" he asked us.

We shook our heads unknowingly. Larry sat down beside me and the three of us began to analyze the meaning of the cards as if they had some kind of hidden message someone was trying to send us.

"These pictures represent the people in our inner circle," Darin theorized as he pointed to several cards: This card here shows the informant."

Together, we began to put real names to the faces on the cards in support of Darin's theory. The faces began to change features before my eyes, becoming more comical and producing laughter from deep inside me. We continued to play until our minds drifted to images created by the light of the chandelier.

Darin pulled a baggy of tie stick from his pocket and loaded the bong. We each took a toke. The mixture of the two drugs in my system induced an extreme hallucinogenic state. Darin put the bong aside, stood on the table and began to turn the chandelier in a circular motion to create different images. Larry and I became enthralled by the melodic sound of his voice as he guided us into another dimension.

The front door slammed, bringing us back from our journey.

"Anyone home?" a deep, soothing voice yelled.

"Yeah, we're in here," Darin responded.

Following the sound of the voice, Rick entered the dining room.

At the sight of Rick, paranoia began to seep into my mind. I had never been afraid of him before. "What's up?" I asked myself. "It must be the tie stick, which traditionally produces this type of effect for me." I sat motionless and speechless while the three men talked. After a short time, I gathered up enough courage to move, without hesitation excused myself and went upstairs to the safety of the bedroom. Larry joined me shortly after I went up.

I lit some candles and plopped down on the bed next to Larry. Staring idly at the ceiling, the glow of the candles began to create images before our eyes and together we deciphered what they were.

"Look," I pointed to the far corner of the room.

"It's a large flower with a bee buzzing near the center. Do you see it? " I asked.

"Yeah, and look over there. A spider is spinning a web."

Light continued to create various images of insects. We laughed at the sight of shadows dancing on the walls until our stomachs hurt. Until weariness set in.

I kissed Larry good night and headed for my room next door. It was unusual that I slept in the room that accommodated my belongings.

As I reached for the door knob Larry spoke, "Where are you going?"

"I'm going to sleep in my room tonight. We need to get some sleep." I wasn't certain why that night was so different. I seemed to be moved by something within myself and I followed.

"O.K. I'll see you in the morning. I love you," he said softly.

"I love you, too."

I shut the door behind me and entered my room. I stripped off my clothes, crawled into bed and drifted off into sleep.

Awakening in an uncanny calm, I lay quietly on my bed until Larry entered my room.

"Good morning," Larry said brightly.

"Good morning, Sunshine."

"Do you mind going with me to the gas station to get some cigarettes and gas?"

"Sure, just give me a minute to throw some clothes on and I'll be right down."

I quickly put on a pair of shorts and T-shirt and met Larry out by my car. As soon as we pulled out of the cul-de-sac onto Brea Canyon road, two sheriff's cars were on our tail.

"You knew this was going to happen, which is why you insisted we get some sleep," Larry said gratefully.

Not quite sure how to respond, I nodded my head.

We continued on Brea Canyon road until we reached Lambert and pulled into the ARCO station on the corner. As we drove in, we noticed three Orange County police cars in line with the Walnut sheriffs. We came to a halt at the pumps. The officers had already parked their cars, and were dispersing with guns pointed at the Camaro. The calmness of my dream still remained inside me. I sat silently waiting for things to unfold, uncertain why all this commotion was taking place.

The officers approached our vehicle, shouting, "Put your hands on the wheel and get out of the car!"

We realized that it was a completely impossible order to obey. How could he possibly step out of the car and keep his hands on the wheel, so we remained seated in the car. Larry placed his hands on the wheel and waited.

An officer appeared at each door and proceeded to open them. "Put your hands on your head and get out the car."

Obediently we followed their orders . Larry was handcuffed. A panicked look entered his eyes.

"Larry Jennings, you are under arrest for assault with a deadly weapon against Robert Trier. You have the right to remain silent........Do you understand your rights?"

"Yes, sir," he replied quietly.

Two officers searched the car inch by inch with a fine tooth comb. They went so far as to remove the carpeting from the floor.

I stood off to the side next to an officer as Larry was placed into the police car and taken away. The officer questioned me about my connection with Larry and about drugs. I managed to remain unruffled while I answered his questions until he made a statement I interpreted as a threat.

"You're fortunate that I don't take you to jail right now. Next time I come across your path, I will. You can leave now."

I stared at the officer as he spoke. Upon his dismissal I returned to my car and drove cautiously back home. What had just happened was finally starting to set in. Larry was in jail and I was afraid for him. A pretty boy like that would be sure to be Big Al's sexual boy toy.

I parked the car in the driveway and ran inside the house. I paced the kitchen floor and tried to gather my thoughts while I waited for Larry to call. The phone rang. I sprinted to the living room where the phone resided and picked up the receiver.

"Hello," I said breathlessly.

"Will you accept a collect call from Larry?" the operator asked.

"Yes!"

"Louise?" Larry asked.

"Yeah it's me," I said.

"You have to get me out of here. The walls are closing in on me," he pleaded.

"I'll do my best, but it may take awhile. I don't know what the bail is or how I'll come up with the money."

"Just do whatever it takes. Use the house for collateral, pawn all the jewelry, whatever it takes. I'll kill myself if I have to spend the night in jail!"

"O.K., O.K., I'll figure out a way to get bail posted by tonight. I love you." With that I replaced the receiver on the cradle.

I called the sheriff's station and found out the bail had been set at $30,000 dollars. The wheels in my head started turning. All creative financing methods leapt to the forefront of my mind. I grabbed the yellow pages, a piece of paper and placed them on the dining room table. I headed upstairs, snatched up all of our jewelry that was of value and returned to the dining room. I put the jewelry on the table and proceeded to bring the telephone in from the living room to the dining room. I made myself comfortable for the beginning of what I knew might be an extremely long day.

I opened the phone book to bail bonds. I began calling the numbers until I found one that would work with me. She educated me on the process and the steps necessary in order to have Larry released.

"In order for a bond to be posted, you have to pay us ten percent of the bail. His bond is $30,000 so you need to have $3000.00. You can use a home or some other possession of value that is worth the bail amount as collateral. Do you have the $3000.00?"

"No, but I can get it. It will just take awhile," I answered

"Do you have collateral?"

"Yes, he owns a home with his sister that has over $100,000 worth of equity."

"O.K. when you have the $3000.00 dollars, call me. I'll come over and we will fill out the necessary paperwork on the house. Bye."

As I was hanging up the phone, a familiar knock rapped on the front door.

"Come in," I yelled. I stood up from the table and walked over to embrace Rick. As usual, he appeared when I needed him most and seemed to instinctually know what was happening inside the walls of Larry's house.

I began to share with him what had happened. " A few days ago when we were all locked up in the house, Larry lost it. Robby was still going about his daily routine, work, etc...He came home and Larry started badgering him about finishing some upholstery work in his truck. Robby said he would get to it when he had time, which was not acceptable to Larry. Larry became upset, and as the argument escalated, so did the ferocity of his anger. They got in a shoving match. Larry pulled a knife on Robby and said "Nobody works me like that." Then he began yelling at him to leave. Robby tried to get some things from his room. Larry struck him with the blunt part of the knife, chipping his tooth and creating other wounds from striking him a number of times. Robby finally got out of the house, but he pressed charges."

Rick was not surprised, and offered help. He would take all the jewelry to the pawn shop while I ran to the bank and withdrew as much cash as I could from my three Visas and would meet me back at the house.

Rick questioned why Larry wasn't willing to wait till the arraignment tomorrow when he could have the bail reduced.

"He's scared and threatening to take his life," I said.

"O.K. Well, if this is what he wants, we'll post bail," Rick responded.

Between the two of us, we were able to come up with the ten percent for the bail bondsman. Larry's sister arrived to sign the paperwork for the bail bond. Since she was the co owner of the house she had to sign it over.

Rick and I followed the bail bonds person to the sheriff's station. When we arrived at the station, night had fallen over the city. Bail was posted. Larry was released. I stayed in the waiting room of the station, anticipating a warm greeting and a show of appreciation. I stood when I saw the door opening. Larry walked through it. He looked at me with little or no acknowledgment, and as he walked past me said, "Let's go." I took stride right behind him out to the car.

Rick was waiting in the car. When he saw us exit the station he stepped out of the car and Larry walked directly to Rick. Larry embraced him and thanked him profusely. Rick glanced over his shoulder and could see the tears welling up in my eyes.

"I didn't do much, it's Louise you owe the gratitude to."

Larry turned to me and kissed me on the cheek and said, "Thanks."

We all got in the car and left. I sat in the back seat with tears streaming down my face. I was disappointed and hurt by Larry's lack of appreciation and affection. Art was waiting at the house with Jan when we returned.

Art was one Larry's oldest friends. They grew up across the street from each other. Art had a handsome, rugged appearance. He had golden hair and blue eyes. Art had just gotten out of jail and had heard through the grapevine of Larry's arrest, and came over to offer some support. Art was also aware that Larry had a room for rent. He decided to seize the opportunity and talk to Larry about moving in. It was decided Art would move in September 1.

Rick set Larry up with a criminal defense attorney and gave him some advice on how to handle his legal problem. Rick had extensive knowledge of the legal system's ins and outs. Larry followed his advice.

About a month after Larry's arrest, Rick came over to the house holding a newspaper article in his hand and told us to read it. I took it from him and read it out loud. It said the Fly had been arrested for drug trafficking, along with two other people I did not know. The article said the drug ring leaders had set up P.O. Boxes in California, Texas and Florida, which was how the product was being transported across the nation. After I finished reading it, we waited silently for Rick's explanation.

"Mike just didn't listen to me when I told him to cool it. So needless to say," he said, whipping out a small baggy of the pink, "This is the last of it. Let's enjoy it."

That was the only thing Rick told us about the arrest. Both Larry and I were disappointed that our supplier was no longer available, but thankful it was him and not us. Along with the arrest of the head people came some peace from the police. It appeared as though they had pulled their troops off the investigation since they could not connect Larry with dealing and had him on other charges now.

The beatings became milder and were almost nonexistent after Art moved in.

Rick quietly faded out of our lives over the next few weeks upon Art's arrival, as if his job had been completed.

Art had a history of physical abuse and had served time for his violent temperament. He came out of jail realizing the wrongs he had committed against women and had learned to focus that energy in a constructive manner. Every time Larry would begin to move towards me in an abusive manner, Art would step in and say ,"If you hit someone, hit me. I'll fight you if that is what you're looking for." Each time he confronted him, Larry would back down. Larry was afraid of Art, and with good reason.

Art had connections in the drug world so he would set up deals for Larry. We continued to drink and drug with our friends that were still around. Art and I grew closer and closer. Our friendship blossomed and I looked at him as an older, protective brother.

Then one night in mid October Larry, decided to go out with the guys, leaving me at home with Art and couple of other friends. I told Larry to have good time and I'd see him later. The four of us played cards and darts, drank beer and did lines. We were having an evening of laughter and fun, until Larry came home. He saw us at the table playing cards, having a good time, and immediately lost his temper.

He moved towards me while screaming obscenities. Just as he was about to hit me, Art placed himself between Larry and me. Art shoved Larry backwards, causing him to stumble.

"What's your problem, dude? You better stay away from her, or you'll have to deal me," he said as Larry was trying to regain his balance.

I ran to the other side of the room in case fists started flying. Our friends just stared at Larry in amazement, letting the scene play out.

"Get the hell out of here, just get the hell out of here! This is my house I want you to leave," Larry hollered at Art.

"Fine, if you want me to leave, I'll leave in the morning. It is the witching hour, and I've been drinking. I'm not about to get in my truck and drive," he reasoned.

"I'll call the police if you don't leave right now," he retorted.

"Call the police if you want, but I'm not leaving tonight," Art replied, never believing Larry would follow through with his threat.

The police arrived. Larry went outside to tell them the situation. The rest of us remained inside the house, but we could hear Larry ranting and raving, outside making no sense.

The police came into the house and suggested that we leave. Art told them that he had a few beers. The cops said they would follow him to his destination to ensure his safe arrival.

I grabbed my purse and I began following Art and our friends out the door. Larry was standing on the staircase with hatred in his eyes, glaring at me. He grabbed my arm as I passed.

"You stay. I just want Art to leave. You stay!" he hissed.

At that moment, I knew if I didn't leave I might never get the opportunity again, because Larry would kill me or beat me so badly I would be unrecognizable. I managed to draw enough inner strength and pull away from him. Without saying good bye, I followed my friends to their car. My car had been repossessed recently so I would ride with Art, leaving all my belongings except my purse behind. I would return to get them at a later time. As we drove down the street that night, a little angel sat on my shoulder telling me it was going to be all right. "You did the only thing you could do if you want to live," the angel said.

-57-

The sound of the Rebel and Misty barking on the other side of the door jolted me back to the present. I pounded my fist on the front door. I fought my impulse to run. I pushed down the feelings of fear that arose in my stomach. I stood solid and still on the front porch, waiting for an answer. I raised my fist to pound again, when the door suddenly flung open.

Larry stood before me. Hatred flamed in his eyes. His skin was almost transparent, revealing every muscle and vein. Without movement or expression in a statuesque pose I remained until I was ready to speak. I would not shrink away from him. He could not hurt me anymore, I reminded myself over and over, until I knew it without a doubting bone in my body.

"I'm here to pick the rest of my things," I said as I stood in front of him, arms wrapped around my body to fight the chill.

"I'm busy!" he replied as he began to close the door.

Turning to leave, I paused and screamed over my shoulder, "Fine, I'll call the sheriff to act as a peace officer. Then we'll see how busy you are!" intending to, and accomplishing a reactive response from Larry. Immediately after the last word left my lips, I ran for my life, across the cul-de-sac towards the ARCO station across the boulevard to the pay phone. I could hear his footsteps thudding against the asphalt as he chased me. The phone was within my reach. He was still a few steps behind me. "I made it." I thought to myself.

As I began to dial, my head suddenly jerked back from a tug on my hair. I felt a sting across my cheek. I dropped the receiver and tried to protect my face. I twisted and turned until I loosened his hold on my hair. Everyone in close vicinity to the gas station could hear the shrill sound of his voice screaming at me.

"Cunt, whore, I'll kill you, hang up the phone, now!" He yanked the phone from my grasp. Firmly gripping both shoulders, he began to shake me as if I was a rag doll, no longer seeming unthreatening. Suddenly, he contained the strength of a man double his size.

I looked around wildly for someone who might help, but the street was vacant. The shop keepers peered out of their windows, wide eyed and unwilling to involve themselves in this domestic dispute. Why should they? I realized I had to help myself. From within me, I withdrew a power that was tougher than steel and mightier than Hercules, as I lifted my foot in one swift kicking motion. The toe of my shoe created a cracking sound as it made contact with his shin. In his surprise at my ability to fight back, he immediately released me.

I ran as fast as my feet would carry me to another pay phone across the way. Grasping for breath, I quickly dialed the Sheriff's number.

"Walnut Sheriff's station. Is this an emergency?"

"Yes," I replied, panting heavily.

"What is the emergency?" the voice asked.

Recounting the situation to the woman on the line, I stressed the urgency of the situation. Within five minutes, a black and white arrived at the phone booth location.

"Did you call about a domestic dispute in progress?" the officer asked.

"Yes."

"Where is the perpetrator now?" they asked.

"At home." I said

"What is his address?"

I gave the officers Larry's address, at the same time the sense of urgency was growing and swirling around inside of me.

I was impatient with the officer's questions and in a rush to show Larry I meant what I said. "What if Larry leaves before we get over there?" I asked myself. I also needed to prove that I was no longer the impish, little rag doll he could terrorize and walk away from, only to do it another day. This would be the last time.

"He needs to be held accountable for his actions and I want my stuff back, now." I blurted out.

" He will be punished for breaking the law, but we have a couple more questions before we can make an arrest. You will get your belongings back after we make the arrest." The officer said scribbling down some notes. "Does he have any weapons in the house?"

" Yes, a gun, a knife and a sword. That is all I know about," I answered, fidgeting with my lighter.

"Has he acted violently towards you before?"

"Yes," I said.

"O.K., let's go. You can ride over with us." The two officers and I got in the car.

The eagerness of the officers to arrest Larry was shown by their actions. I was escorted back to the house and told to wait beside the car. The officers knocked on the front door, identifying themselves. No answer came from inside the house. The only noises were those of the dogs barking wildly.

"Open the door or we'll break it down. We'll kill your dogs if they get in our way," they shouted through the door with guns drawn.

Relief and satisfaction surged through me as I watched the officers make their presence known to Larry.

The door screeched open. "I was in the shower, what is the problem?" Larry asked looking bewildered at the officers.

Stepping towards Larry they said "You are under arrested for spousal abuse. Place your hands on top of your head, now." In California, the domestic violence laws dictated that if a couple cohabited they were considered spouses, which brought with it a heavier punishment for the perpetrator.

Placing his hands on top of his wet hair, he seemed to shrink before my very eyes. I had moved closer to the door, in order to hear what was going on. The officer noticed me behind them and turned to speak to me. "Would you find Mr. Jennings a shirt, for old time sake?"

Maneuvering around them, I darted upstairs and grabbed an old T-shirt, stopping on the landing and looking down in a glorious moment of victory. "This is what it must feel like to win the gold at the Olympics." I speculated to myself. I tossed the T-shirt down to the officer and watched. Larry stood motionless, his body sagging, shoulders hunched over, head bowed to the floor as if praying to a God he never knew. He had lost his power over me. Over his life. The T-shirt was slipped over his head and his arms placed through the sleeves by the officers.

"Place your arms behind your back." The silver handcuffs clicked coldly as they were tightened around his wrist. Their polished shine glimmered in my eyes, creating joy throughout out every cell of my being like a ray of sunshine would after a long Seattle winter. Without taking my eyes off the cuffs I strolled down the stairs and continued to the front door. I noticed that beneath the violent, hateful carcass of this man, fear flashed in his eyes. While reading Larry his rights, they escorted him to the car. As he passed me, spittle sprayed from his mouth like a venomous poison, but I was already immune. The saliva landed on my cheek and with intense rage in his eyes he hissed," This isn't over, you'll pay for this."

I met his words with an equal amount venom darting from the look in my eyes. A case where the old cliché "if looks could kill, you'd be dead," definitely applied. The officers placed him in the back seat and pulled away from the curb. My body trembled with relief. I relished the idea of him behind bars. He would not hurt me or anyone else again. A shattered shell of a woman laid at my feet. From the debris arose a child; determined, angry, and fighting to be free. I stood alone on the porch and triumphantly raised and thrust my arms into the air and screamed "Yes!" I did not wither away at the cruelty in which he spoke or acted. My desire to live and stop merely surviving overtook me with a zest that was unexplainable and to place words on this feeling would only limit the excitement that radiated from within me. The excitement that came with making the choice to change.

That night I slept in a peaceful slumber.

My eyes adjusted slowly to the brightness that began to penetrate the darkness I found myself in. The light filtered in slowly, bringing with it a warmth to my flesh, my heart and my soul. I turned my head slowly in all directions, looking for the creature that had tormented and haunted me in the confines of the basement. The light cast a glimmer in the corner where I could see a deformed, shriveled appendage lying on the concrete floor. Unable to move my eyes from the sight of it for fear it come alive and steal me back into its blackness, I watched. It disintegrated into a pile of dust as I stared in awe. A breeze began to blow. The dust dispersed into nothing and with its disappearance I stood and walked into the light.

My life was my own. It was nothing less than miraculous to watch the sun rise the following morning without the fear of being beaten. As I watched the sun rise, I thanked God for my life and asked for guidance on my new path.

Epilogue

The Captain anchored the hundred twenty foot yacht off the coast of British Columbia, in a majestic area he called Kit bay. The Crew and I finished our duties just before the sun was setting in the sky over Canada. Exhausted from the previous ten days of cooking, cleaning, and serving ten guest, that had departed only a few hours prior, my ship mates returned directly to their quarters when the chores were finished. I walked outside and leaned against the bow railing and raised my head towards the sky, relishing the solitude of the moment. It was eleven thirty at night when the sun began its descent. A large cumulous cloud hung off in the distance. I noticed two distinct openings in the cloud. The openings were almond shaped, through them the radiance of the sunset beamed. The rays touched my skin with their warmth in the coolness of the July evening. Silently I said to myself, the eyes of God are shining upon me. I pulled my scarf tight around my neck as chills streamed from my head to my toes, I continued to look at the beauty before me. The tears streamed down my face, I curved my lips upward and my soul smiled.

I had begun to lay the mortar for my foundation with no specifications on design or dimension, only plenty of room for expansion. I felt a hand touch my shoulder. I turned around to see Sam standing in front of me, our live aboard fishing expert, a medicine man among his people and my friend.

He said, "As your heart is open let it always remain. That is where all the answers to your questions lie and that is where the creator within each of us lives. For the Creator does not make mistakes.

I reached for his hands and took them in mine. I looked into his eyes not only to see his beauty, but to see the reflection of my own. Graciously I thanked him for his friendship and the teachings he had shared with me during our journey together. When I fell silent his hands slipped away from mine and he began to sing in his native language. He sang a beautiful prayer to Great Spirit, the four directions, mother earth and father sky. Standing reverently I silently said a prayer of thanks as the divine words of prayer vibrated through the night air. Sam finished, we embraced.

I jotted down the date, July 7, 1994 as I always did when I made an entry in my journal. I began writing, when without fore thought, what flowed from my pen was no longer what I had experienced or felt that day, but a story of four years past, a story of abuse, addiction, death, life, triumph and miracles.

ABOUT THE AUTHOR

Born of Hungarian descent, in Pasadena California, in March of 1967. Autumn's childhood was turbulent, although as a child, she would find solace in communion with plants, trees, spiders, birds, nature she seemed to be in natural alignment with mother earth.
She attended school all the way through college in Southern California, where she was an above average student. She is an accomplished scuba diver and massage therapist, among other things. And this is not her first attempt at writing. For Autumn is a published poet, with the ability to reach right into the heart of life and put into words what many of us have difficulty communicating.

A relationship that could be characterized as a "school of hard knox" was the fire that forged her into this awesome, loving, strong woman she had become today. I am honored to be her friend and I feel that once you have read her book you will understand why.

About the Author was written by G.W.Taylor.